Jung's Last Years and Other Essays

THE JUNGIAN CLASSICS SERIES

serves to make available again works of long-standing value in the tradition of C. G. Jung's psychology:

Aniela Jaffe
Apparitions
An Archetypal Approach to Death Dreams and Ghosts

James Hillman
Insearch
Psychology and Religion

Marie-Louise von Franz
The Passion of Perpetua

Victor White
God and the Unconscious

Edgar Herzog
Psyche and Death
Death-Demons in Folklore, Myths and Modern Dreams

Robert Stein
Incest and Human Love
The Betrayal of the Soul in Psychotherapy

Aniela Jaffé

Jung's Last Years
and Other Essays

Translated by R. F. C. Hull
and Murray Stein

Spring Publications, Inc.
Dallas, Texas

The first four chapters of *Jung's Last Years and Other Essays* were originally published by Rascher & Cie, Zurich, © 1968 as *Aus Leben und Werkstatt von C. G. Jung* and published under the English title *From the Life and Work of C. G. Jung*, Harper & Row, N.Y., 1971, from whom the typography of this edition has been gratefully acquired. The Standard Book Number for the Harper Colophon Edition was 06–090169–1; the Torchbook Library Edition had SBN: 06–136044–9 and Library of Congress Catalog Card Number: 73–154656.

The fifth chapter of the present edition was published originally in the *Eranos Yearbook–40*, 1971, pp. 85–122, E. J. Brill, Leiden, Holland, and in the present English translation by Murray Stein in *Spring 1972 (An Annual of Archetypal Psychology and Jungian Thought)*.

Printed in the United States of America by BookCrafters, Inc., Chelsea, Michigan, for Spring Publications, Inc., P.O. Box 222069, Dallas, Texas 75222

International Distributors:
Spring/Postfach/8800 Thalwil/Switzerland; Japan Spring Sha, Inc./31, Shichiku-Momonomoto-Cho/Kitaku, Kyoto, 603 Japan; Element Books Ltd/ The Old Brewery Tisbury Salisbury/Wiltshire SP3 6NH/England

Cover design and production by Intentions Advertising:
Patricia Mora and Maribeth Lipscomb.

Library of Congress Cataloging in Publication Data

Jaffe, Aniela.
Jung's last years and other essays.

(Jungian classics series)
Translation of: Aus Leben und Werkstatt von C.G. Jung.
Reprint. Originally published: Harper & Row, 1971.
With new last chapter.
1. Jung, C. G. (Carl Gustav), 1875–1961. 2. Psychoanalysts–Switzerland–Biography. I. Title. II. Series.
BF173.J85J4413 1984 150.19'54 [B] 83–20419
ISBN 0–88214–505–3

Contents

	Preface	vii
I.	Parapsychology: Experience and Theory	1
	Occultism and Spiritualism	
	Synchronistic Phenomena	
II.	Alchemy	46
III.	C. G. Jung and National Socialism	78
IV.	From Jung's Last Years	99
V.	The Creative Phases in Jung's Life	138

Preface

A peculiarity of Jung's scientific method was that he would constantly return to the basic problems in his writings, examine them from different points of view, think through old questions again, and give new and differentiated answers. This makes a reading of his works an exciting experience, but at the same time it complicates a thorough understanding of a particular problem. So it is only natural that his collaborators and pupils have repeatedly been asked to clarify one or another of his themes.

In 1965 Professor J. R. Smythies of the University of Edinburgh asked me to contribute an essay on Jung's experiences and researches in the field of parapsychology for the symposium *Science and ESP*, in the International Library of Philosophy and Scientific Method.[1] The first essay, "Parapsychology: Experience and Theory," is an expanded version of that contribution.

Jung's parapsychological researches form one of the most difficult, but from the scientific point of view most important, chapters of his work. The explanatory principle of synchronicity which he put forward as complementing causality enabled us to understand many hitherto inexplicable phenomena and to fit them into a scientific framework. Thanks to his

1. J. R. Smythies, *Science and ESP* (London, 1967).

insights parapsychology became the bridge between the psychology of the unconscious and microphysics.

Jung liked to turn his attention to out-of-the-way and disquieting problems on the ground that security, certitude, and peace do not lead to discoveries. Parapsychology was just such a problem, and in many eyes it still is today. The same is true of alchemy. Jung recognized, however, not only that the beginnings of chemistry are to be found in the labors of the alchemists, but that the contents of the alchemical texts must be regarded as a mystico-religious world of images and ideas springing from the unconscious. This arcane aspect constitutes the importance of alchemy for depth psychology.

The Bollingen Foundation, New York, commissioned me to write an essay, "The Influence of Alchemy on the Work of C. G. Jung," for the catalogue of the Mellon Collection, *Alchemy and the Occult.*[2] "Alchemy" is a revised and expanded version of that essay. In 1921 Paul Mellon and his first wife, Mary Conover Mellon, had begun collecting works from alchemical and occult literature. Their interest had been aroused by conversations with Jung. After the death of Mary Mellon, Paul Mellon kept adding to the collection until it was completed some twenty-five years later. It comprises about three hundred works, as many books as manuscripts. In 1965 he bequeathed it to the Yale University Library, which has since (1968) brought out a two-volume, copiously illustrated catalogue of the books in an edition of five hundred copies. The catalogue cites for comparison Jung's use of the material in his writings and also the books he owned, a collection of about two hundred items.

In 1966 Colonel Laurens van der Post encouraged me to take up the much-discussed theme of Jung's attitude to National

2. Compiled by Ian Macphail, with essays by R. P. Multhauf and Aniela Jaffé and additional notes by William McGuire, 2 vols. (New Haven, 1968).

Socialism. Van der Post was shocked by the constantly repeated charges that Jung had been a Nazi and an anti-Semite; he had known Jung too well to give them any credence. An account of the facts—those that speak in his favor as well as those that weigh against him—as seen in historical perspective, together with a psychological interpretation, seemed to van der Post and to me the best way of countering these attacks. I have tried to give such an account in the third essay which, like the fourth, is published here for the first time in English.

I wrote the last essay, "From Jung's Last Years," at the request of numerous people who, though familiar with his scientific writings, also wanted a picture of his personality. Their request was understandable since Jung had become something of a legend even during his lifetime—a curious fact which the posthumously published *Memories, Dreams, Reflections*[3] did nothing to dispel. That book was concerned almost exclusively with the experiences of the "inner man"—Jung called him Personality No. 2—but there was little about Personality No. 1, who had his roots in the outside world and in human relationships. My essay attempts no more than to present an impromptu series of snapshots of Personality No. 1, sidelights on the last years of Jung's life. Many others would have to be added to round out the picture of the man.

ANIELA JAFFÉ

3. C. G. Jung, *Memories, Dreams, Reflections,* recorded and edited by Aniela Jaffé, translated by Richard and Clara Winston (New York and London, 1963).

Jung's Last Years and Other Essays

I.

Parapsychology: Experience and Theory

Occultism and Spiritualism

To Carl Gustav Jung parapsychology was more than a subject for scientific research, experiment, and theory. His life was rich in personal experiences of spontaneous, acausal, or—to use the common term—paranormal phenomena. He seemed to be endowed with an unusual "permeability" to events in the background of the psyche. But that alone does not explain the scope of his experiences; his sensitivity to manifestations of the unconscious was supplemented by constant observation of nature, of objects, and of people. Given his close attention to the worlds of the psyche and of external reality, it is not surprising that he perceived meaningful connections between the two which would have been overlooked by a less sharp observer. Prophetic dreams and precognitions were no rarity in Jung's life, though far from habitual. Whenever they occurred he noted them with surprise—one is tempted to say, with the awe due to the miraculous. He gave a circumstantial account of them in his memoirs,[1] written when he was in his eighties.

1. *Memories, Dreams, Reflections,* recorded and edited by Aniela Jaffé, translated by Richard and Clara Winston (New York and London, 1963).

Jung's mother, Emilie Jung (née Preiswerk, 1849–1923), had a similar gift and was interested in the "supernatural." She left behind a diary in which she noted down all the premonitions, "spookish" phenomena, and strange occurrences she had experienced. Her father, Samuel Preiswerk (1799–1870), was head of the reformed clergy in Basel, and as a child she was often assigned the task of protecting him from "spirits." She had to sit behind him when he was writing his sermons, because he could not bear "spirits" passing behind his back and disturbing him. Every week, at a fixed hour, he used to hold intimate conversations with his deceased first wife, very much to the chagrin of the second! Jung's psychiatric diagnosis was that he suffered from "waking hallucinations," though at the same time he dismissed this as a "mere word." Samuel's second wife, Augusta (née Faber, 1805–1862), Jung's maternal grandmother, was gifted with "second sight" and could also see "spirits." The family traced this back to an episode when, as a young girl, she lay for thirty-six hours in a state of catalepsy resembling death. Her gifts, however, could stand the test of a more rigorous judgment: she sometimes saw apparitions of persons unknown to her, but whose historical existence was later proved.

Jung's interest in parapsychology as a science began when he was studying medicine, that is, in the last years of the nineteenth century, when terms like "somnambulism" or "spiritualism," popularized by the Romantics, were much in vogue. One of his old school friends, Albert Oeri,[2] wrote in an essay dedicated to Jung on the occasion of his sixtieth birthday:

> I will not deny that Jung underwent a severe test of personal courage when he studied spiritualistic literature, did a

2. Later, member of the Swiss Parliament and editor of the daily newspaper *Basler Nachrichten.*

> good deal of experimentation in that field, and stood by his convictions unless they were modified by more careful psychological studies. He was up in arms when the official science of the day simply denied the existence of occult phenomena instead of investigating and trying to explain them. Thus spiritualists like Zöllner and Crookes, whose theories he could discuss for hours, became for him heroic martyrs of science. Among friends and relatives he found participants for spiritualistic séances. . . . I enjoyed enormously listening to Jung holding forth on this subject when I came to see him in his lodgings. His charming dachshund would look up at us so gravely, as if he understood everything, and Jung used to tell me that the sensitive little creature sometimes whimpered piteously when some occult force manifested itself in the house.[3]

As Oeri indicates, Jung did not confine himself to reading "occult" literature, but began his own experiments and, during the years 1899 and 1900, organized regular séances. The medium was one of his cousins, a fifteen-year-old schoolgirl. At the beginning of this enterprise, two "occult" phenomena took place in the house he was sharing with his widowed mother and sister. A heavy walnut table, an old heirloom, split with a loud report, and soon afterwards a bread knife in a sideboard inexplicably snapped into four pieces, again with a sound like a pistol shot. The four pieces of the knife are still in the possession of the Jung family.[4]

At the suggestion of Professor Eugen Bleuler, later Jung's chief at the Burghölzli Clinic, Zurich, Jung wrote his doctoral dissertation on the results of his spiritualistic experiments. It is entitled "On the Psychology and Pathology of So-called Occult Phenomena."[5] In the context of his work as a whole, this dissertation is of particular interest because it contains the

3. In *Die kulturelle Bedeutung der komplexen Psychologie*, edited by the Psychology Club, Zurich (Berlin, 1935).
4. *Memories, Dreams, Reflections*, pp. 105–6.
5. In *Psychiatric Studies* (Collected Works, 1; hereafter CW).

germs of some of Jung's later concepts which are of basic importance. While lying in a trance, the young medium would utter the words of "personalities" which Jung interpreted as personifications of unconscious "part-souls." This suggested that the psyche was a plurality, or rather, a multiple unity; the part-souls or unconscious parts of the personality anticipated the concept of "autonomous complexes" in the unconscious. This concept soon took on more solid form, mainly through Jung's studies in word association[6] while working as assistant physician at the Burghölzli (1900–1902). It was then that he recognized the autonomous complex as one of the most important factors in the dynamics of unconscious processes. The other concept of basic importance dealt with in his dissertation is the compensatory relation between the conscious and the unconscious. Jung observed that the flood of fantasies and the personified complexes that manifested themselves in the trances complemented the conscious attitude of the medium and aimed at a greater completeness of her character. Above all, it was the regular appearance of an aristocratic and distinguished woman who, as a kind of unconscious ideal, compensated the obviously too simple and unformed character of the young girl.

After a period of intense collaboration the somnambulistic abilities of the medium declined, and she tried to make up for the fruitlessness of the séances by fraud. At this point Jung broke off his experiments. Later, however, the complex of that "higher personality" actually established itself in real life: the unstable young girl turned into a mature and self-reliant woman. Though she died young, at the age of twenty-six, she found a vocation which allowed her to develop her artistic abilities.

6. In *Experimental Researches* (CW, 2), in preparation. *Cf.* "A Review of the Complex Theory," *The Structure and Dynamics of the Psyche* (CW, 8).

It is a well-observed fact that somnambulistic phenomena of a significant nature occur most frequently during puberty. In his dissertation Jung offered the hypothesis that they represent attempts at character development, anticipating a process of differentiation. In many cases they are

> simply new character formations, or attempts of the future personality to break through [which], in consequence of special difficulties (unfavorable circumstances, psychopathic disposition of the nervous system, etc.) get bound up with peculiar disturbances of consciousness. In view of the difficulties that oppose the future character, the somnambulisms sometimes have an eminently teleological significance, in that they give the individual, who would otherwise inevitably succumb, the means of victory.[7]

Thus Jung attributed to somnambulisms the same meaning that he later ascribed to the neuroses: he detached them from the causal viewpoint and posed the question of their final significance within an individual process of development.

In the light of Jung's later work, it is of interest that a genuine mandala came into existence during the reports of the medium's trances. Arranged as a series of concentric circles, it represented a sort of Gnostic system of the cosmos and its energies, which the young girl said she had "received from the spirits" and which Jung drew at her dictation.[8] The production of the mandala formed the climax of the medium's manifestations, and thereafter her utterances became increasingly shallow and meaningless.

Although Jung's active interest in parapsychology never diminished, he did not speak again of his investigations into "so-called occult phenomena" until very much later, when, in 1919, he delivered a lecture to the British Society for Psychical

7. *Psychiatric Studies*, par. 136.
8. *Ibid.*, par. 65, and Fig. 2, p. 40.

Research on "The Psychological Foundations of Belief in Spirits."[9] In this paper he explained spirits and other occult phenomena as unconscious autonomous complexes which appear as projections, or, in other words, as "the exteriorized effects of unconscious complexes," thus taking up again the argument of his dissertation. He went on:

> I for one am certainly convinced that they are exteriorizations. I have repeatedly observed the telepathic effects of unconscious complexes, and also a number of parapsychic phenomena, but in all this I see no proof whatever of the existence of real spirits, and until such proof is forthcoming I must regard this whole territory as an appendix of psychology.[10]

When the paper appeared in revised form in 1948, almost thirty years later, Jung added a footnote to this sentence, based on the new conception he had formed of the collective unconscious, the archetypes, and hence also of occult phenomena:

> After collecting psychological experiences from many people and many countries for fifty years, I no longer feel as certain as I did in 1919, when I wrote this sentence. To put it bluntly, I doubt whether an exclusively psychological approach can do justice to the phenomena in question. Not only the findings of parapsychology, but my own theoretical reflections outlined in "On the Nature of the Psyche"[11] have led me to certain postulates which touch on the realm of nuclear physics and the conception of the space-time continuum. This opens up the whole question of the transpsychic reality immediately underlying the psyche.

The theoretical reflections to which Jung here alludes will be discussed below in greater detail. But we may anticipate to

9. In *The Structure and Dynamics of the Psyche.*
10. *Ibid.*, par. 600 and p. 9, n. 15 below.
11. In *Ibid.*

this extent: he had come to the conclusion that beyond the world of the psyche with its causal manifestations and relations in time and space (that is, beyond consciousness and the personal unconscious) there must lie a transpsychic reality (the collective unconscious) where, as one of its main characteristics, a "relativation" of time and space occurs, and where, consequently, the law of causality loses its absolute validity. What consciousness experiences as past, present, and future is relativized in the unconscious until they merge "there" into an unknowable unity, or timelessness; and what appears to consciousness as near and far undergoes the same process of relativation until they combine "there" into an equally unknowable spacelessness. In investigating the discontinuities in subatomic processes, physics has also been confronted with the problem of acausality and the relativation of time and space, and this is of significance as regards the position of Jung's discoveries and hypotheses within the framework of modern science.

Concurrently with his recognition of a transpsychic reality there went a differentiation in his conception of the archetypes, which must be regarded as the contents, or vehicles, of that transconscious realm. From 1946 onward, Jung described them as "psychoid,"[12] which means that they are not purely psychic but just as much physical in nature. This contamination, running parallel with the contamination of the space-time categories in the unconscious, is an obvious paradox, though it is no more baffling than the familiar paradox of light in physics, which under some conditions must be explained as consisting of waves and under others, of particles.

The psychoid archetype is not to be confused with archetypal images or archetypal contents. These belong to the knowable realm of consciousness and occur as analogous mo-

12. *Cf.* "On the Nature of the Psyche," *Ibid.*, pars. 368, 420, 439.

tifs in myths, fairy tales, dreams, delusions, etc., at all times and in all parts of the world. The psychoid archetype, or "archetype per se," is an unknowable factor in the collective unconscious, which underlies those motifs and arranges them into typical images and groupings. It is a structuring element, comparable to a "pattern of behavior" in biology, that also underlies typical and recurrent situations in life, such as birth, death, illness, change, love, and, operating like an instinct, preforms typical relationships such as those between mother and child, husband and wife, teacher and pupil, and so on. Jung compared the archetype per se to the "axial system of a crystal, which, as it were, preforms the crystalline structure in the mother liquid, although it has no material existence of its own."[13]

Since the archetype per se is psychoid, Jung succeeded in showing that it also arranges acausal parapsychological events (prophetic dreams, precognitions, etc.), thus opening the way to an understanding of these hitherto inexplicable phenomena. The relationships between the two will be discussed in greater detail in the section on synchronistic phenomena below.

The postulate of an unknowable psychoid world in the background alters our initial question concerning the nature of spiritualistic phenomena only to the extent that Jung was no longer able to maintain with certainty his original thesis that spirits are exteriorizations or projections of autonomous psychic complexes. What they really are, where they come from, why and where they are seen, remained for him—at least in most cases—a baffling question that could not be answered conclusively, and so it remains for science to this day.[14] He expressed himself very cautiously in his foreword to the Ger-

13. "Psychological Aspects of the Mother Archetype," *The Archetypes and the Collective Unconscious* (CW, 9, Part I), par. 155.
14. *Cf.* A. Jaffé, *Apparitions and Precognition* (New York, 1963).

man edition of Stewart Edward White's *The Unobstructed Universe*[15]: "Although on the one hand our critical arguments cast doubt on every single case [of apparitions], there is on the other hand not a single argument that could prove that spirits do not exist. In this regard, therefore, we must rest content with a *non liquet*."

In his contribution to Fanny Moser's book, *Spuk: Wahrglaube oder Irrglaube?*[16] Jung describes his own encounter with a ghost in England in 1920. He spent several weekends in a friend's recently rented country house. During the nights he experienced various increasingly violent ghostly phenomena like knockings, evil smells, sounds of rustling and dripping. They aroused in him a feeling of suffocation and a sensation of growing rigidity, and culminated in the apparition, or hallucination, of a solid-looking half of a woman's head lying on the pillow about sixteen inches away from his own. Its one eye was wide open and staring at him. The head vanished when Jung lit a candle. He spent the rest of the night sitting in an armchair. He and his friend later learned what was already known to the whole village: the house was haunted and all tenants were driven away in a very short time.

Jung interpreted some details of his experience as exteriorizations of psychic contents in the unconscious. But what remained an insoluble puzzle was the fact that the haunting took place solely in that house, indeed, in one particular room of the house. During the week when he stayed in London, he slept peacefully in spite of a heavy working schedule. It was a typical case of localized haunting, for which to this day no adequate scientific explanation has been found. The house was pulled down shortly after Jung's visit.

15. *Das uneingeschränkte Weltall* (Zurich, 1948). The Foreword is included in CW, 18, in preparation.

16. (Baden bei Zurich, 1950). Jung's contribution is included in CW, 18.

In the early twenties Jung, together with Count Albert Schrenk-Notzing and Professor Eugen Bleuler, carried out a series of experiments with the Austrian medium, Rudi Schneider, at the Burghölzli. They witnessed materializations, psychokinetic and other phenomena. Jung conducted similar experiments in the thirties with the medium O. Schl., again in the presence of Bleuler and others. Jung told me later that in one series of experiments, papier-mâché objects (cutouts of angels and beer mats) which had been covered with luminous paint and placed out of reach of the medium rose up in the air and sailed through the room as soon as the medium fell into a trance.

Twenty-five years later, when Jung was in Central Africa, he was reminded of those experiments by a typical chain of associations. On the train journey from Mombassa to Nairobi, he beheld a brownish-black figure who stood motionless on a steep red cliff, leaning on a long spear and looking down at the train.

> I was enchanted by this sight—it was a picture of something utterly alien and outside my experience, but on the other hand a most intense *sentiment du déjà-vu.* I had the feeling that I had already experienced this moment and had always known this world which was separated from me only by distance in time. . . . The feeling-tone of this curious experience accompanied me throughout my whole journey through savage Africa. I can recall only one other such recognition of the immemorially known. That was when I first observed a parapsychological phenomenon together with my former chief, Professor Eugen Bleuler. Beforehand I had imagined that I would be dumbfounded if I were to see so fantastic a thing. But when it happened, I was not surprised at all; I felt it was perfectly natural, something I could take for granted because I had long since been acquainted with it.[17]

17. *Memories, Dreams, Reflections*, pp. 254–55.

In 1961, the year of his death, looking back on the phenomena he had observed, Jung wrote in a letter:

> I have seen objects moving that were not directly touched, and moreover under absolutely satisfactory scientific conditions. One could describe these movements . . . as levitation, if one assumes that the objects moved by themselves. But this does not seem to be the case, because all the bodies that apparently moved by themselves moved as though lifted, shaken, or thrown by someone's hand. In this series of experiments I, together with other observers, saw a hand and felt its pressure—apparently the hand that caused all the other phenomena of this kind. The phenomena have nothing to do with the "will," since they occurred only when the medium was in a trance and precisely not in control of his will. The phenomena seem to fall into the category of poltergeist manifestations.[18]

According to a later report of Jung's it was a child's hand he had seen and whose pressure he had felt. After a time it faded away.

Jung was a critical observer, not susceptible to suggestion. At one séance, four of the five people present saw an object like a small moon floating above the abdomen of the medium. It was absolutely incomprehensible to them that Jung, the fifth person, could see nothing of the sort, although they repeatedly pointed out to him exactly where it was.[19] From this Jung inferred the possibility of collective visions on such and other occasions—for instance, the sightings of flying saucers.[20]

When he was asked by Professor Fritz Blanke of Zurich, author of a book on Niklaus von der Flüe, the patron saint of Switzerland, for an explanation of the saint's twenty-year fast from 1467 to 1487, he reverted to the experiments at the

18. See p. 95, n. 42 below.
19. *Cf.* "Flying Saucers: A Modern Myth of Things Seen in the Skies," *Civilization in Transition* (CW, 10), par. 597.
20. *Ibid.*

Burghölzli, in particular the materialization processes. It was not impossible, he wrote in his answer,[21] that the nourishment of the saint was effected in a parapsychological way. He himself had been present at the investigation of a medium who manifested physical phenomena. It was found that at one point on the body where there was an emission of ectoplasm capable of acting at a distance, the ionization of the atmosphere in the immediate vicinity of the medium was about sixty times the normal. At that point, therefore, ionized molecules were going in and out through the surface of the body. Apparently it is these molecules that lead to the formation of the whitish or luminous ectoplasmic mist and also of materialized bodily parts. "If such things can occur," wrote Jung, "then it is also conceivable that persons in the vicinity of mediums might act as a source of ions—in other words, nourishment might be effected by the passage of living molecules of albumen from one body to another." His hypothesis is supported by the fact that "in parapsychological experiments decreases of weight up to several kilograms have been observed during the [physical] phenomena, both in the case of the medium and of some of the participants, who were all sitting on scales." But Jung did not commit himself in these reflections, seeing in them merely a possible approach to an explanation of the miraculous fast. "Unfortunately these things have been far too little investigated. This is a task for the future" was the conclusion of his letter.

In later years Jung no longer concerned himself with spiritualistic or occult phenomena and he never evaluated his parapsychological experiments scientifically, yet he did not by any means dismiss them as worthless. "Although I have not distinguished myself by any original researches in this field, I

21. "Das Fastenwunder des Bruder Klaus," *Neue Wissenschaft* (Oberengstringen, Switzerland), 1950/51, Heft 7. "The Miraculous Fast of Brother Klaus" is included in CW, 18.

do not hesitate to declare that I have observed a sufficient number of such phenomena to be completely convinced of their reality. To me they are inexplicable, and I am therefore unable to decide in favor of any of the usual interpretations."[22] His interest in these matters brought him, above all, an enrichment of experience entirely in accord with his scientific attitude as an empiricist. "In this vast and shadowy region, where everything seems possible and nothing believable, one must oneself have observed many strange happenings and in addition heard, read, and if possible tested many stories by examining their witnesses in order to form an even moderately sure judgment," he says in his foreword to Fanny Moser's book. This sentence might stand as a motto to Jung's work in the field of parapsychology.

The space-timeless realm of "transpsychic reality" naturally tempts one to any number of speculations and hypotheses not only about spirits but also about a Beyond and a life after death. Jung personally held the opinion that man would miss something essential if he did not reflect on these matters and even indulge in fantasies about them. His life would be poorer, his old age perhaps more anxiety-ridden, and furthermore he would break with a spiritual tradition that reaches back to the dawn of human culture. From earliest times death and the idea of a life after death have filled man's thoughts, and in religion, philosophy, and art have prompted answers to what is rationally unanswerable. To throw all this to the winds is, from the psychological standpoint, symptomatic of an atrophy of instinct and a willful disregard of one's psychic roots, both of which must be paid for dearly. Death remains a terrifying darkness and becomes an enemy.

But if man forms opinions about death and the Beyond he

22. Foreword to Stewart Edward White, *Das uneingeschränkte Weltall.*

should never forget that he is entering the world of myths. Salutary and beneficial though these may be, they nevertheless have nothing to do with science, or rather, since all science grew out of myth, do not *yet* have anything to do with it. In his memoirs, the chapter "On Life after Death" is devoted to Jung's fantasy thinking or "mythologizing": "Even now I can do no more than tell stories—'mythologize.' "[23] He offered a scientific answer that set bounds to mythological thinking in his essay "The Soul and Death" (1934).[24] Here he stressed the fact that the psyche extends into a spaceless and timeless sphere, for which reason it is also capable of extrasensory perceptions. This would provide sufficient grounds for speculation but would not permit of any final conclusions about a postmortal existence. A year before his death he expressed himself with somewhat greater precision on the same theme. In a letter of May 1960, he wrote that in so far as the psyche is capable of telepathic and precognitive perceptions it exists, at least in part, in a "continuum outside time and space," hence the possibility of authentic postmortal phenomena.

> The comparative rarity of such phenomena suggests at all events that the forms of existence inside and outside time are so sharply divided that crossing this boundary presents the greatest difficulties. But this does not exclude the possibility that there is an existence outside time which runs parallel with existence inside time. Yes, we ourselves may simultaneously exist in both worlds, and occasionally we do have intimations of a twofold existence. But what is outside time is, according to our understanding, outside change. It possesses relative eternity.

Finally, a word should be said about a class of experiences, familiar to scientists, which in the English literature on the

23. *Memories, Dreams, Reflections*, p. 299.
24. In *The Structure and Dynamics of the Psyche.*

subject are called the "out-of-the-body-experiences." In a condition of profound unconsciousness, with the brain completely inactive, a person can have experiences about which he is able to report on returning to consciousness and which can be verified down to the smallest detail. Occasionally he is able to perceive future events, and not infrequently he can observe his own body from outside, lying there as if lifeless. In *Man's Concern with Death*,[25] edited by Arnold Toynbee, the chapter by R. Heywood is devoted to these reports. They form the starting point for a discussion of the continued existence of the soul after death, which these out-of-the-body-experiences seem to bring within the realm of the conceivable.

In his paper "Synchronicity: An Acausal Connecting Principle,"[26] Jung reports on a number of such experiences, including one presented by Sir Auckland Geddes to the British Society of Medicine.[27] The conclusion he draws, or rather the hypothesis he advances, has, however, nothing to do with parapsychology in the proper sense; moreover, it does not lead on to a discussion of the possibility of life after death. Jung takes as his starting point the researches of Karl von Frisch into the life of bees, in particular the "bee language," through which they communicate to their comrades, by means of a peculiar sort of dance, the direction and distance of the feeding places they have found.[28] The information so conveyed must be regarded as "intelligent" and is understood by the bees. Yet insects have no cerebrospinal system at all, but only a double chain of ganglia corresponding to the sympathetic system in man. Jung concludes that the ganglionic system can evidently produce thoughts and perceptions just as easily as the cerebrospinal system. He asks,

25. London, 1968.
26. In *The Structure and Dynamics of the Psyche.*
27. *Ibid.*, pars. 949–54.
28. Karl von Frisch, *The Dancing Bees*, translated by D. Ilse (New York and London, 1954).

> What then are we to think of the sympathetic system in vertebrates? Von Frisch's observations prove the existence of transcerebral thought and perception. One must bear this possibility in mind if we want to account for the existence of some form of consciousness during an unconscious coma. During a coma the sympathetic system is not paralysed and could therefore be considered as a possible carrier of psychic functions. If that is so, then one must ask whether the normal state of unconsciousness in sleep, and the potentially conscious dreams it contains, can be regarded in the same light—whether, in other words, dreams are produced not so much by the activity of the sleeping cortex, as by the unsleeping sympathetic system, and are therefore of a transcerebral nature.[29]

In his memoirs Jung describes an out-of-the-body-experience of his own which he had while in a state of deep unconsciousness during a severe illness in 1944.

> It seemed to me that I was high up in space. Far below I saw the globe of the earth, bathed in a gloriously blue light. I saw the deep blue sea and the continents. . . . My field of vision did not include the whole earth, but its global shape was plainly distinguishable and its outlines shone with a silvery gleam through that wonderful blue light. . . . Later I discovered how high in space one would have to be to have so extensive a view—approximately a thousand miles! The sight of the earth from this height was the most glorious thing I had ever seen.[30]

Today, a quarter of a century later, it is tempting to take this as a precognition of the experience of the astronauts as, themselves "out-of-the-body" of this world, they gazed in wonder at the shining blue planet, Earth, rising over the moon's horizon.

29. *Ibid.*, par. 957.
30. *Memories, Dreams, Reflections*, chap. X, "Visions," pp. 289–90.

Synchronistic Phenomena

Of far more importance for Jung's scientific work than the occult or spiritualistic phenomena we have been discussing (ghosts, and the question of life after death), were certain causally inexplicable events generally summed up as extrasensory perceptions. They play a role in premonitions, prophetic dreams, inspirations, telepathy, precognitions, and "hunches" as well as in "mantic" methods of astrology, geomancy, the tarot cards, and the Chinese *I Ching, or Book of Changes.*[31] The literature and traditions of all countries and ages abound in examples of extrasensory perception, describing them as strange and miraculous occurrences and as evidence of the "supernatural" powers of men and animals.

In most of these experiences an unknown event inaccessible to the sense organs is perceived as an inner, psychic image (for instance, in a dream or vision). It does not matter whether the event perceived has actually taken place in the past, is taking place in the present, or will take place in the future; nor is it of any importance whether it happens nearby or in some remote part of the globe. *It is perceived here and now.* Usually these strange coincidences of inner image and outer event are looked upon as mere chance. But that does not explain them. Jung had a skeptical attitude towards the all-too-liberal use of the concept "chance" in science. He backed up his objections by reminding his critics of Freud, for whom "chance" slips of the tongue, pen, or memory became the starting point for important psychological discoveries. Moreover, a scientific explanation of extrasensory perception is doomed to failure so long as it is based on the principle of causality. How can an event in

31. The German translation by Richard Wilhelm, rendered into English by Cary F. Baynes (New York, 1950, 2 vols.; 3rd ed. in 1 vol., 1968).

the future be the cause of a dream that is taking place in the present, so that it reflects itself and is anticipated in it? How can a man dying in New York cause a person somewhere in Europe to have a premonition of his death, let alone cause a clock to stop or a glass to shatter? To put it more simply and realistically, how can the subject of a test score a probability-exceeding result when he tries to "perceive" the sequence of twenty-five picture cards which are uncovered one after another by the experimenter in a different room? But that is precisely what J. B. Rhine of Duke University has statistically demonstrated in his famous card experiments.[32] They proved conclusively that man possesses a paranormal capacity for extrasensory perception.

Jung based his theoretical researches into parapsychology largely on the positive results of Rhine's experiments, which have lent reality a new dimension.[33] "Rhine's experiments have taught us," he says, "if practical experience has not already done so, that the improbable does occur, and that our picture of the world only tallies with reality when the improbable has a place in it."[34] For the purposes of scientific inquiry, the improbable is of greater importance than that which is probable from the start.

Parapsychology has been endeavoring for a long time to establish the reliability and veracity of reports of spontaneous extrasensory perceptions which were not experimentally induced and observed. This it has succeeded in doing in a large number of cases, especially when a prophetic dream, premonition, etc., was reported or recorded in writing *before* the event

32. For a brief account of the experiments, see Jung, "Synchronicity: An Acausal Connecting Principle," in CW, 8, *The Structure and Dynamics of the Psyche*, pars. 833ff.

33. *Cf.* Rhine, *Extra-Sensory Perception* (Boston, 1934), and *New Frontiers of the Mind* (New York and London, 1937).

34. "Flying Saucers," par. 744.

it "perceived." Since numerous proofs of their veracity exist today and have been published in the literature on the subject, and most of the experiences exhibit, furthermore, some degree of similarity, we no longer have to rely, as in the early days of parapsychology, on the verification of each single case. Even so, the problem of confirmation remains. In cases where dreams are systematically recorded, as in the course of an analysis, verification is often made very much easier.[35]

The chief objection to the scientific tenability of parapsychological phenomena still rests today on the impossibility of a causal explanation. For the thinking of Western man, it is almost insuperably difficult to give up the principle of causality—regarded as absolutely valid since the time of Descartes—and to accept the reality of acausal connections. The entry on parapsychology in the *Encyclopædia Britannica* (1961 edition) makes this perfectly clear: "The chief obstacle to a more widespread scientific acceptance of the findings of parapsychology, as some of the fairest and most competent sceptics have pointed out, is the almost complete lack of any plausible theoretical account as to the underlying causal process." But science was the first to break down the absolutism of the causal principle. Once it had accepted the statistical validity of natural laws, then logically it had to take account of the exceptions brought to light by the statistical method. This put an end to the absolute validity of causality, above all in the observation of processes in the borderline territories of the infinitely great (the cosmic realm) and the infinitesimally small (the subatomic realm). Jung established a corresponding situation in the realm of psychology: in the case of irregular processes which are conditioned not only by consciousness but also by the unconscious "the connection of events may in certain cir-

35. *Cf.* C. T. Frey-Wehrlin, ed., "Ein prophetischer Traum," *Spectrum Psychologiae* (Zurich, 1965), pp. 249ff.

cumstances be other than causal, and requires another principle of explanation."[36]

Jung called this other principle that supplements causality "synchronicity," and defined it as "a coincidence in time of two or more causally unrelated events which have the same or a similar meaning."[37] It is an empirical concept that "merely stipulates the existence of an intellectually necessary principle which could be added as a fourth to the recognized triad of space, time, and causality."[38] Jung expressly emphasized, however, that the principle of synchronicity should be applied only when a causal explanation is unthinkable. "For, whenever a cause is even remotely thinkable, synchronicity becomes an exceedingly doubtful proposition."[39]

Jung's definition has led to frequent misunderstandings because "coincidence in time" is generally understood as an astronomical simultaneity dependent on clock time. It is, rather, a *relative simultaneity*, to be understood as the subjective experience of an inner image coinciding with an outer event. Only in this experience is the time difference abolished, since the event, whether in the past or future, is immediately present. It may happen that inner image and outer event are connected together by an objective, clock-time simultaneity, but that is not the decisive factor. The decisive factor lies in a subjectively experienced, relative simultaneity, for which reason Jung chose the term synchronistic rather than synchronous, and spoke of synchronicity and not synchronism.

Swedenborg's vision, reported by Kant,[40] of a conflagration

36. "Synchronicity," par. 819.
37. *Ibid.*, par. 849.
38. *Ibid.*, par. 958.
39. *Ibid.*, par. 876.
40. In *Dreams of a Spirit-Seer, Illustrated by Dreams of Metaphysics*, trans. by E. F. Goerwitz (London, 1900), Appendix II, pp. 155ff. This Appendix reproduces Kant's letter to Charlotte von Knobloch, mentioned below.

in Stockholm while he was fifty miles away in Göteborg comes into the category of synchronous events, since the vision and the fire coincided in time. Nevertheless Jung would call it a synchronistic phenomenon because of its acausality. But when Goethe, after parting from Friederike Brion, saw his double riding towards him, "not with the eyes of the body but of the spirit," a future event was immediately present: eight years later Goethe rode back along the same way to visit Friederike, wearing, to his own amazement, the same attire, "smoky grey with some gold," that had struck him on encountering his double.[41] Experiences of the past as immediately present seem to be rarer or to have been reported less frequently. Great excitement was aroused by the experience of two English schoolteachers, C. A. E. Moberly and E. F. Jourdain, who in 1901 visited the park in Versailles. Wandering near the Petit Trianon, they fell into a dreamy state marked by an unusual feeling of anxiety, and had hallucinatory encounters with figures from the time of the French Revolution. They observed details of the layout of the garden, details which had vanished when the hallucinatory state came to an end, but which could subsequently be verified from the old plans and charts. The precise notes the two ladies took of their strange experience were published in 1911 as a book with the title *An Adventure*.[42]

Kant's report of Swedenborg's vision of the fire in Stockholm, which took place in the year 1759, shows the almost insurmountable difficulty of accepting acausal phenomena as true and valid. Even that towering thinker was not quite equal to the task! He had given an account of the episode in a letter, of uncertain date, to Charlotte von Knobloch, adding that a

41. *Cf. Goethe, Dichtung und Wahrheit*, 1811–14, Part 3, Book 11.
42. Republished with an introduction by E. Olivier and a Note by J. W. Dunne (London, 1948). *Cf.* also A. Jaffé, *Apparitions and Precognition*, pp. 120ff.

friend of his had checked it and found everything confirmed by eyewitnesses both in Stockholm and Göteborg. There was no question of his doubting Swedenborg's vision. His *Dreams of a Spirit-Seer* was published in 1766, and here he expresses himself with much more reserve. Again the facts are faithfully reported, but he as good as apologizes for serving up such a "fairy tale" and leaves it to the reader's discretion, "faced with the wondrous tale with which I have admixed myself, to resolve into its elements that ambiguous mixture of reason and credulity, and to calculate the proportion of the two ingredients in my manner of thinking."[43] In the very next sentence he says that he deems himself "sufficiently secured against mockery," since by criticizing "this foolishness" he finds himself "in right good and numerous company." Collective thinking, then as now, is opposed to the instinctive knowledge of unsophisticated people who have always experienced such happenings and taken them seriously, just as it is opposed to the scientist who sets out to replace the habitual categories of thought by new ones.

Synchronistic phenomena are not characterized only by the relative simultaneity we have been discussing. According to Jung's definition, a decisive role is also played by their *meaning*. It is meaning, or the sensing of a meaningful connection, that condenses acausally connected events into a single, integral experience. Frequently the meaning emerges from the similarity or actual equivalence of the inner and outer event. Jung gives an example of this. At the very moment when a patient was telling him a dream about a golden scarab, a scarab-like beetle, a rose-chafer, tapped gently against the outside of the windowpane.[44] Here two distinct events (dream of the

43. *Dreams of a Spirit-Seer,* Part Two, Section 1.
44. *Cf.* "Synchronicity," par. 843.

scarab, appearance of the rose-chafer), each with its own chain of causality, are connected together only by the equivalence of motif, by meaning.

Sometimes an unexpected encounter with a child, an animal, an object, or the sight of a landscape, a falling leaf, an everyday scene, or any other incident can mirror the inner event in the most precise way, and may even repeat an image seen in a dream. Such contemplative experiences of the meaningful equivalence of inside and outside are likewise based on synchronicity. Generally they arouse a sense of wonder, sometimes also of tranquility or liberation, possibly connected with an intimation of oneness with the world, of being held safely in the arms of life itself.

The equivalence of content whereby meaning is experienced can become an almost photographic repetition or anticipation of an external event by an inner image. Someone chances to come to a strange city and finds his way about with no difficulty and without a guide. He recognizes everything, because sometime before he had wandered through its streets and squares in a dream. It is probable that the *sentiment du déjà-vu* arises from anticipatory but forgotten dreams.

In many cases the synchronistic equivalence is expressed only indirectly, and then it is a symbolic connection that evokes the experience of meaning. This is true, for example, of those strange parapsychological happenings in which an object plays a part: it is meaningful that a clock suddenly stops, a mirror breaks, a glass shatters, a door opens by itself to "announce" the death of a friend or relative, as folklore has it, for all these happenings can be interpreted as symbols of death. The same is true of dreams: the dream-image of a falling tree, of a person walking along who cannot be caught up with, of a blinding light or a light being extinguished, can herald death just as much as the dream of a journey or of bidding someone farewell. Always it is the conformity of content that connects the psychic and physical facets of a synchronistic phenomenon.

Occasionally dreams are reported of a character so strange and weird that only one who is familiar with archetypal imagery can recognize their symbolic kernel as a herald of death. In the last essay he wrote before he died, Jung recapitulated the salient points in a dream series of an eight-year-old girl.[45] She had written the dreams down in a little book which she gave to her father as a Christmas present when she was ten; she died a year later. The dreams portray in great archetypal images impersonal, religious, and philosophical problems that far exceed the understanding of an eight-year-old girl. The little girl's account of her dream about the "bad animal" ran:

> Once upon a time I saw in my dream an animal that had lots of horns. It spiked up other little animals with them. It wriggled like a snake and that was how it lived. Then a blue fog came out of all four corners, and it stopped eating. Then God came, but there were really four Gods in the four corners. Then the animal died, and all the eaten-up animals came out alive again.[46]

The symbolic meaning places the foreseen or intuited death in a timeless, mythological setting. The religious creativity and mythopoeic faculty of the psyche are here at work.

Every prophetic dream, every premonition has its own psychic causality, independent of any other causal chain leading up to the event which is "perceived" in them. The con-

45. "Approaching the Unconscious," in the symposium *Man and his Symbols* (London, 1964), pp. 70–71.

46. Contained in Jung's seminar "Psychologische Interpretation von Kinderträumen," 1939/40, at the Federal Polytechnic Institute, Zurich (mimeographed stenographic record for private circulation). The dream is reproduced in "A Study in the Process of Individuation," *The Archetypes and the Collective Unconscious*, par. 623, and discussed at length in Jolande Jacobi, *Complex/Archetype/Symbol* (London and New York, 1959), pp. 139ff.

necting link between the inner and outer event is, as we have said, meaning. Yet it should not be forgotten that it is man who experiences and assigns meaning, that it depends on man whether phenomena of this kind are dismissed as mere chance, as vapid and nonsensical, or are simply overlooked. For this reason it is of paramount importance that Jung, in pursuing his investigation of synchronistic phenomena, ranged alongside the concept of meaning the objective, scientific concept of an "acausal orderedness," a comprehensive order, independent of man, which underlies acausal events and connects them. We shall come back to this later.

It was characteristic of Jung's restraint in scientific matters that he waited more than twenty years before presenting to the public his revolutionary essay on synchronicity. In 1952 it appeared together with an essay, "The Influence of Archetypal Ideas on the Scientific Theories of Kepler,"[47] by the physicist and Nobel prizewinner Wolfgang Pauli. Jung had coined the term synchronicity and had used it for the first time in his memorial address for Richard Wilhelm[48] in 1930, when he sought to explain the methods of the Chinese oracle book, the *I Ching, or Book of Changes,* dating from the fourth millennium B.C.

In the early twenties he had come across the *I Ching* in the English translation by James Legge.[49] Greatly fascinated, he experimented with it for a whole summer. At first he used the complicated procedure in which the forty-nine yarrow stalks have to be divided and counted off according to fixed rules. Later he used the simpler coin method: three coins are thrown six times, each throw giving one of the six lines that constitute the "hexagram," of which there are sixty-four in all. To each

47. *Cf.* Jung-Pauli, *The Interpretation of Nature and the Psyche* (New York and London, 1955).

48. "Richard Wilhelm: In Memoriam," *The Spirit in Man, Art, and Literature* (CW, 15).

49. *The Yi Ching* (Sacred Books of the East, 16; Oxford, 1882).

line is appended an oracle text with a commentary. The positive and meaningful answers that Jung and his friends got from the hexagrams confronted him with the unsolved problem of the mantic methods mentioned earlier.

In a foreword to the new English translation of the *I Ching*, written very much later (1948), Jung justified his much-derided interest in this seemingly out-of-the-way territory:

> The irrational fulness of life has taught me never to discard anything, even when it goes against all our theories (so short-lived at best) or otherwise admits of no immediate explanation. It is of course disquieting, and one is not certain whether the compass is pointing true or not; but security, certitude, and peace do not lead to discoveries. It is the same with this Chinese mode of divination.[50]

According to modern theoretical physicists, belief in a quantitative, mechanistic picture of the world has turned out to be more and more of a superstition.[51] For this reason even parapsychology, at least in its most important branches, is recognized by them as a legitimate field for scientific research. Indeed, Wolfgang Pauli has actually described it as the "border territory between physics and psychology."[52]

For Jung's researches into parapsychology, and especially the mantic methods, it was a momentous event when he became acquainted with Wilhelm in 1928. Their first meeting, which soon developed into a friendship, took place when Wilhelm, with the help of his learned friend Lau Nai Süan in China, had after ten years of work just completed a new translation of the *I Ching*, along with a commentary on the oracles.

50. "Foreword to the *I Ching*," *Psychology and Religion: West and East* (CW, 11), par. 1000.

51. *Cf.* W. Heitler, *Der Mensch und die naturwissenschaftliche Erkenntnis* 3rd ed. (Braunschweig, 1964), pp. 96–97.

52. Wolfgang Pauli, "Naturwissenschaftliche und erkenntnistheoretische Aspekte der Ideen vom Unbewussten," *Dialectica* (Neuchâtel), Vol. 8, 4, pp. 283–301.

In frequent discussions the two scholars exchanged ideas about the book and the interpretation of its hexagrams, so strange to the Western way of thinking. In memory of these talks Jung wrote:

> I owe to Wilhelm the most valuable elucidations of the complicated problem of the *I Ching* and also the practical evaluation of the results obtained. . . . When Wilhelm was staying with me in Zurich, I asked him to work out a hexagram on the state of our Psychological Club. The situation was known to me, but to him not at all. The diagnosis that resulted was startlingly correct, and so was the prognosis, which described an event that occurred later and that I myself had not foreseen. To me personally, however, this result was no longer so amazing, since I had earlier already had a number of remarkable experiences with the method.[53]

It is exceptional for the answers given by the *I Ching* to contain actual prophecies. Far more frequently they are symbolic descriptions of a psychological situation that is unclear to the questioner because he is unconscious of it. Jung says of the *I Ching:* "Like a part of nature, it waits until it is discovered. It offers neither facts nor power, but for lovers of self-knowledge, of wisdom—if there be such—it seems to be the right book."[54] After the experimental period of the twenties had passed, and Jung was no longer so filled with scientific curiosity about the *I Ching*, he consulted it only rarely, and then only when it seemed opportune to seek an answer to a specific question in a specific situation. Politeness to the spirit of this venerable book demands such restraint, only a fool importunes it, says one of the oracles (hexagram 4: Youthful Folly). A specific situation presented itself when Jung was asked to

53. This passage is not contained in the English version of the Foreword to the *I Ching*, but only in the unrevised German original, reproduced in Gesammelte Werke, 11, *Zur Psychologie westlicher und östlicher Religion*, pp. 634–35.

54. "Foreword to the *I Ching*," par. 1018.

write the foreword to the new English edition. He then consulted the book twice, first asking it what it had to say about his intention to write a foreword, and then, after the foreword was half written, whether his action had been right. His analysis of the answers takes up nearly three-quarters of the foreword. The unprejudiced reader cannot but admit that the *I Ching*'s answers were both wise and meaningful.

In his memorial address for Richard Wilhelm, Jung summed up his explanation of the divinatory method in terms of his newly coined "synchronistic principle."

> The science of the *I Ching* is based not on the causality principle but on one which–hitherto unnamed because not familiar to us–I have tentatively called the *synchronistic* principle. My researches into the psychology of unconscious processes long ago compelled me to look around for another principle of explanation, since the causality principle seemed to me insufficient to explain certain remarkable manifestations of the unconscious. For I found that there are psychic parallelisms which simply cannot be related to each other causally, but must be connected by another kind of principle altogether. This connection seemed to lie essentially in the relative simultaneity of the events, hence the term "synchronistic."[55]

Jung explained the positive results of the *I Ching* oracles as synchronistic phenomena, that is as an "unexpected parallelism of psychic and physical events."[56] There is a meaningful connection (through equivalence) between the subjective and objective situation of the questioner and the hexagram resulting from the fall of the coins, which reflects that situation. Yet no regular concurrence should be expected between the hexagram and the inner and outer reality. It would also be a

55. "Richard Wilhelm: In Memoriam," par. 84.
56. See p. 27 n. 53 above and Gesammelte Werke, 11, p. 638.

senseless undertaking to try to demonstrate any such regularity, since much depends on whether the questioner understands the meaning of the oracles, veiled as they are in symbols and difficult to interpret, and on whether he feels the answers to be apposite or "right."[57] Jung himself inclined to the belief, without being able or even wishing to prove it, that "right" answers "are not a matter of chance at all but of regularity."[58] This personal belief is at odds with his own scientific theory that synchronistic phenomena should under all circumstances be regarded as irregular occurrences. His belief would be explained or justified by the fact that he consulted the *I Ching* only in critical situations, which, as will be shown, are the prerequisite for acausal phenomena.

In the course of explaining the *I Ching* Jung also touched on the question of the foundations of astrology, in particular of character horoscopy, a mantic method widely in use today. Originally he regarded astrology as a function of time: just as a connoisseur can tell with absolute certainty the vintage and provenance of a wine, so a good astrologer can tell a person to his face in what zodiacal signs sun, moon, and ascendent stood at the moment of his nativity. Such knowledge is possible because time is not, as is generally supposed, only an abstract concept and a conditioning factor of cognition, but must be understood as a "stream of energy filled with qualities,"[59] so that the time quality peculiar to the moment of a man's birth also attaches to his character and possibly to his fate as well.

The old astrological stellar myths are expressions of these

57. "Foreword to the *I Ching*," par. 974. As Jung says (*ibid.*), the hexagram "reveals its meaningful nature only if it is possible to . . . verify its interpretation, partly by the observer's knowledge of the subjective and objective situation, and partly by the character of subsequent events."

58. See n. 53 above and Gesammelte Werke, 11, p. 635.

59. Letter, January 1934.

intuitively grasped time qualities. They are archetypal images, involuntary creations of the "knowing unconscious," which primitive man projected upon the stars. Jung wrote in a letter (June 1960):

> We must bear in mind that we do not make projections, rather they happen to us. This fact permits the conclusion that we originally read our first physical, and particularly psychological, insights in the stars. In other words, what is farthest is actually nearest. Somehow, as the Gnostics surmised, we have "collected" ourselves from out of the cosmos.

The conception of astrology as a function of the time quality deflates the argument which, more than any other, is leveled against the seriousness and justification of astrology as a science; namely that, owing to the precession of the equinoxes, the astronomical position of the constellations in the zodiac no longer corresponds to the astrological zodiac on which horoscopes are calculated. A word of explanation may be necessary here. The point where the sun rises on March 21st, the vernal equinox, is called the "spring-point." In the second century B.C., Hipparchus of Samos fixed it at 0° Aries. The precession is the slow movement of the spring-point through the twelve zodiacal signs along the ecliptic, from Aries to Pisces to Aquarius, etc. It takes 25,200 years (a "Platonic year") for the spring-point to make a complete revolution of the zodiac, and rather more than 2000 years (a "Platonic month") for it to move through each zodiacal sign. At the beginning of our era it advanced from Aries into the first degrees of Pisces, and since about the middle of the present century it has been crossing over from Pisces into Aquarius.

So if in the birth horoscope of a man living today the sun stood in Pisces, by astronomical reckoning it was not in Pisces but in Aquarius; if it was astrologically in Aquarius, astronomically it was in Capricorn, and so on. How then can a horoscope be right?

The astronomical objection to astrology would be justified if the horoscope was actually based on the stars and their influence. But according to Jung's original view, it is not a question of any influence exerted by the stars and their positions, not a question of causality but of synchronicity; that is, of the peculiar quality of the moment of birth, as portrayed in myths and archetypal images, and its acausal coincidence with the inner and outer events in a man's life. "Whatever is born or done at this particular moment of time has the quality of this moment of time."[60]

Jung explained the difficult concept of time qualities by means of an example. The astrological fixing of the time "sun in Aries" (correlated with March and April) has the quality "spring," and it is springtime "regardless of the actual astronomical zodion in which the sun stands. In a few thousand years, when we say it is Aries time, the sun will actually be in Capricorn, hence in deep winter [in a winter sign], although the spring will not have lost its powers."[61] The quality of the time moment March/April, or of the astrological statement "sun in Aries," is and remains spring. The astronomical positions of the stars are merely quantities named by man for measuring and determining time but do not tell us anything about its qualities. It is a hoary old peasant rule that domestic animals born in spring and autumn display typical differences of character.

In 1951 Jung's synchronistic theory of astrology began to waver. That year Max Knoll delivered a lecture at the Eranos meeting in Ascona, Switzerland, on "The Transformations of

60. "Richard Wilhelm: In Memoriam," par. 82.
61. See p. 29,n. 59 above. Additions in brackets by A. J.

Science in Our Age."[62] He pointed out that the proton radiation from the sun is influenced to such a degree by the conjunctions, oppositions, and quartile aspects of the planets that the occurrence of electromagnetic storms (sunspot periods) can be predicted with a fair amount of probability. And since correspondences have been established between sunspot periods and the mortality rate, as well as disturbances of "radio weather" during those periods, there is a real possibility of causal connections and direct influences. These astronomical observations have confirmed the unfavorable influence of planetary conjunctions, oppositions, and quartile aspects, as always assumed by astrology, and the positive influence of the astrologically favorable trine and sextile aspects.[63]

The scientific discovery of these causal relationships gave Jung an unexpected glimpse into the theoretical foundations of astrology. At first he was inclined to repudiate its inclusion among the mantic methods based on synchronicity, for, according to the new findings, the possibility of a causal connection between the planetary aspects and man's psychophysiological disposition would have to be taken seriously into account. "Astrology," he said, "is in the process of becoming a science."[64]

Later Jung revised this somewhat too drastic or one-sided statement and opined that synchronistic as well as causal connections would have to be adduced in explaining astrology. In April 1958 he wrote in a letter: "Astrology seems to require differing hypotheses, and I am unable to opt for an either-or. We shall probably have to resort to a mixed explanation, for nature does not give a fig for the sanitary neatness of our intellectual categories of thought."

62. In *Man and Time*, Papers from the Eranos Yearbooks (Bollingen Series XXX; London and New York, 1957).

63. *Cf.* "Synchronicity," par. 875.

64. "On Synchronicity," *The Structure and Dynamics of the Psyche*, Appendix, par. 988.

At all events, the positive results obtained with the help of traditional astrological methods of interpretation raise questions which have still not been satisfactorily answered today. After the death of Jung, science made no further endeavors to solve the problem.

Jung's book *Aion* (1951) can, depending on one's standpoint, be regarded either as an astrological treatise or as the proof of a synchronistic phenomenon of cosmic proportions. It is, in part, an account of the meaningful coincidence of the Platonic month of Pisces—which started two thousand years ago with the birth of Christ and, as we have said, is now passing into the Platonic month of Aquarius—with the spiritual development of Christianity during this period. The fish is an old symbol for Christ. The parallelism between the cosmic event—the progression of the spring-point through the double sign of the Fishes—and the spiritual and historical events is exceedingly impressive. The turn of the first millennium, just about the time when the spring-point reached the beginning of the second Fish, witnessed the rise of the heretical movements that compensated and also undermined Christianity—the Cathars, Waldenses, Albigenses, the Holy Ghost Movement of Joachim of Flora, and other sects. Although the year 1000 did not mark the expected end of the world, it secretly initiated the "kingdom of the second Fish"—traditionally interpreted as the age of Antichrist—whose culmination, no one will deny, we are experiencing in the present century.

Jung's method of approaching parapsychological phenomena was to combine extensive studies of the relevant historical and modern literature with careful observation of the inner and outer data presented by individual cases. In astrology Jung not only carried out a statistical experiment himself but called for a statistical evaluation of astrological statements.[65] In

65. "Synchronicity," chap. 2: "An Astrological Experiment."

general, however, statistics for Jung were of secondary importance. In his foreword to Fanny Moser's book he wrote:

> It is true that with the help of the statistical method the existence of such [synchronistic] effects can be proved with more than sufficient certainty, as Rhine and other investigators have done. But the individual nature of the more complex phenomena of this kind forbids the use of the statistical method, as it proves to be complementary to synchronicity and necessarily destroys the latter phenomenon, which statistics are bound to eliminate as probable and due to chance. We are thus entirely dependent on well observed and well attested individual cases.[66]

The question of the circumstances propitious to synchronistic phenomena offers special difficulties. Empirically, it has been established that they occur (in the form of prophetic dreams, premonitions, psychokinesis, etc.) with greater frequency in the vicinity of archetypal events, such as death, illness, crises, the onset of mental diseases. Since in archetypal situations man usually reacts with strong emotions, it would seem that emotion itself favors the occurrence of synchronistic phenomena. And, in fact, during or because of emotion, the threshold of consciousness is lowered, and the unconscious and its contents—the archetypes—gain the upper hand. In other words, man falls into the relative space-timelessness of the unconscious where he experiences synchronistic events more easily than he would in a state of calm and sober consciousness. For this reason paranormal phenomena play a much greater part in the lives of primitives, with their still feebly developed consciousness which is not yet sharply divided from the unconscious, than they do in ours; hence, also the highly developed gift for extrasensory perception occasionally observed in children diminishes when they grow up and their consciousness has become firmly established.

66. *Spŭk: Wahrglaube oder Irrglaube?* p. 11.

In the famous collection of parapsychological cases which Edmund Gurney, Frederic Myers, and Frank Podmore published at the end of the nineteenth century under the title *Phantasms of the Living*,[67] it was shown that most spontaneous parapsychological phenomena were observed in connection with dying and death. This observation was confirmed during the following decades. Death is an archetypal situation of intense numinosity. Here the unconscious breaks through into life, and no one in the vicinity can escape its power, which in many instances affects even animals. The emotion with which the psyche reacts causes a weakening or loosening of the structure of consciousness: prophetic dreams, premonitions, apparitions step through the gaps as heralds of the mighty archetype Death.

The thesis of a connection between emotion and acausal occurrences is historically very old. One of its earliest proponents was Albertus Magnus (1193–1280), who assumed an *excessus affectus* (excess of affect) as the cause of magical influence. Jung inclined to the view that so-called "genuine magic" as practiced by medicine men is based on the scientifically still-unexplained capacity to rouse oneself to a pitch of extreme emotion by an act of will, thus creating the necessary conditions for synchronistic events.[68] The same voluntary immersion in a state of inner excitement seems to underlie the well-known "excursions of the soul," in which conscious measures are taken for a doubling of the personality.[69]

In his memoirs Jung records a synchronistic phenomenon that he himself experienced in a state of great emotion. In 1909 he visited Freud in Vienna. He was interested to hear Freud's views on precognition and on parapsychology in general, and

67. London, 1886, 2 vols.
68. "Synchronicity," pars. 859–60.
69. *Cf.* A. Jaffé, *Apparitions and Precognition*, pp. 157ff.

asked him what he thought about them. Freud dismissed the whole subject as nonsensical. Jung writes:

> While Freud was going on this way, I had a curious sensation. It was as if my diaphragm were made of iron and were becoming red-hot—a glowing vault. At that moment there was such a loud report in the bookcase, which stood right next to us, that we both started up in alarm, fearing the thing was about to topple over on us. I said to Freud: "There, that is an example of a so-called catalytic exteriorization phenomenon."
>
> "Oh come," he exclaimed. "That is sheer bosh."
>
> "It is not," I replied. "You are mistaken, Herr Professor. And to prove my point I now predict that in a moment there will be another such loud report!" Sure enough, no sooner had I said the words than the same detonation went off in the bookcase.
>
> To this day I do not know what gave me this certainty. But I knew beyond all doubt that the report would come again. Freud only stared aghast at me.[70]

Jung was in a highly emotional state, his diaphragm a "glowing vault." Evidently his consciousness had fallen into the sphere of relativized time in the unconscious, and the coming event communicated itself to him as something immediately known.

In many cases, however, the emotion is connected only with the inwardly perceived image of an event (a death, an accident), while the person seeing or anticipating it extrasensorially remains in a relaxed mood. This fact throws light on the nature of synchronistic phenomena. On closer examination it turns out that emotion as such is only a secondary symptom. It may be present in the person who perceives the event, or it may be connected with what is perceived, or it may be missing

70. *Memories, Dreams, Reflections,* pp. 155–56.

altogether. What is essential for the occurrence of synchronistic phenomena is the constellation of an archetype, and emotion is a determining factor only in so far as it brings the unconscious, and hence the archetype, into the foreground.

Synchronistic phenomena and archetypal events are inseparably connected. Since we are accustomed to thinking in causal categories, it is tempting to mistake the archetype for the phenomena's transcendental *cause*. Such a conclusion rests on the same error that leads primitives to explain virtually everything that happens in life as the effect of "magical causality." In reality the archetype must be regarded as the "arranger" of synchronistic phenomena. *It is their condition, not their cause.* The "unexpected parallelism of psychic and physical events" is a manifestation of the archetype's psychoid (psychophysical) nature: because of its "transgressivity,"[71] its psychoid nature is split, and it appears here as a psychic image and there as an external event, occasionally even as a physical object. The archetype arranges itself, along with its antinomies, in the facets of the synchronistic phenomenon. But this split is never so radical that the experience of their underlying unity is lost; indeed, on that depends the experience of meaning, which is the distinguishing mark of synchronistic events.

As we know, a thing becomes conscious only when it becomes distinct from another thing. Consequently synchronistic phenomena, in which parallel psychic and physical events are distinct from each other yet are connected by their equivalence and thus form a meaningful whole, must be regarded as the coming-to-consciousness of an archetype. In general, coming-to-consciousness is an intrapsychic process: the characteristic distinction of one thing from another takes place in the thoughts, dreams, and intuitions of an individual. It

71. "Synchronicity," par. 964.

is different with synchronistic phenomena. Here the antinomies or parallelisms, the various facets of the archetype that is coming to consciousness, are torn asunder. They manifest themselves, psychically and nonpsychically, at different times and in different places. This strange behavior may be explained by the fact that the psychoid archetype has not yet become fully conscious, but exists in a state that is half unconscious and half conscious. It is still partly in the unconscious, hence the relativation of time and space. But partly it has penetrated into consciousness, hence the splitting of its psychoid nature into two or more psychic and physical parallel events that are distinct from one another. This nascent coming-to-consciousness is so thoroughly peculiar and puzzling that our reason struggles against recognizing the conformity of events which belong together. Yet in the border territories of the psyche, that is to say, wherever the unconscious intervenes, we can no longer count upon the clear and logical connections which are mandatory in the world of consciousness.

In most cases it is not difficult to discern the particular archetypal situation underlying or arranging a synchronistic phenomenon. Very often, as we have said, it is death, the imminence of danger, an accident. In the incident between Jung and Freud it was the impending end of a close friendship. It can also, as in the case of the mantic methods, be the expectation of a miracle, the knowing of the unknowable. Jung considered that such an expectation formed the archetypal background of Rhine's experiments. As a rule the score of successes falls off when boredom sets in, when the emotional expectation loses its intensity and the constellated archetype sinks back into the unconscious. Even in apparently banal synchronistic events it is possible in most cases to uncover the organizing archetype. Louisa Rhine, in her book *Hidden*

Channels of the Mind,[72] tells of a young girl who correctly foresaw that she would eat something uncooked, like spaghetti, and another girl unknown to her would say, "That'll swell up in you." If we bear in mind the curiosity, the greed, that prompted her to eat directly from a packet of Lipton's Chicken Noodle Soup, we can discern once again the emotion behind the impulse, while the words "food," "hunger," "eating" give us a clue to the archetypal background. They denote a primordial instinct equal in importance to sex. Both food and sex are deeply rooted in the unconscious and play a role in the formation of archetypal images in myth and religion. They appear as the gods of food and love, and in this form represent the spiritual side of instinct. Instinct and image are facets of one and the same archetype. Our example also contains an unwitting allusion to the old mythological or archetypal idea of impregnation by eating ("That'll swell up in you.").

Telepathy must also be understood as a synchronistic phenomenon, though what happens here is the duplication of a psychic content—which appears both in the sender and in the receiver—rather than the parallelism of a psychic and a physical event. From the psychological point of view, however, the question of sender and receiver is secondary. Fundamentally, both are mere instruments of the autonomous archetype and its arrangement in space and time, or again they may be understood as co-protagonists in the drama of an archetypal situation. Man, his conscious thinking and his will, are pushed into the background, for the impersonal, acausal process of "arranging" (the duplication of a thought in two persons distant from one another) can take place even if nothing is consciously "sent." If on occasion a thought seems to have been transmitted deliberately, it is not an act of will on the part of

72. New York, 1961, pp. 221–22.

the sender that brings it about but the emotional involvement of the individual or individuals, which in its turn is a symptom of the constellated archetype.

The well-known and often astonishing telepathy between mother and child deserves special mention. The mother-child relationship represents an archetypal situation par excellence. For a long time after the birth the two form a psychophysical (and later a psychic) unity, and normally a strong psychic bond persists throughout childhood. It has its roots as much in the unconscious as in consciousness. Hence a much smaller impetus is needed for synchronistic phenomena than with people between whom the unconscious bond is weaker, and who are not contained in one and the same archetypal situation.

Another human relationship in which the unconscious bond is stronger than usual because the partners are involved in an archetypal situation is that between analyst and analysand. It rests upon the (one-sided or mutual) projection of unconscious contents, a phenomenon which Freud called "transference."[73] In such transference relationships—based on an archetype and thus closer to the unconscious—it takes less to constellate a synchronistic phenomenon than with people who are not involved in an archetypal situation: knowledge of one partner concerning the thoughts and experiences of the other is more easily established because they may be drawn more readily into the relativation of time and space.[74]

Synchronistic phenomena have their place midway between the conscious and the unconscious, between the knowable and the unknowable, or between this world and what Jung called

73. *Cf.* Jung, "The Psychology of the Transference," *The Practice of Psychotherapy* (CW, 16).

74. *Cf.* C. A. Meier, "Projection, Transference, and the Subject-Object Relation," *The Journal of Analytical Psychology* (London), Vol. IV, No. 1 (January 1959), and Celia Green, "Analysis of Spontaneous Cases: 'Agent/Percipient Relationships,'" *Proceedings of the Society for Psychical Research* (London), Vol. 53 (November 1960), pp. 108–9.

the "transcendental psychophysical background."[75] Consciousness and this world represent, so to speak, an exfoliation of everything which in that background must be thought of as existing in a state of coalescence and thus forms an unknowable unity. Timelessness divides into past, present, and future; spacelessness into the various dimensions of space; and the unimaginable psychophysical unity of the background realm—more precisely, of the psychoid archetype—appears split into psychic and physical events. In the synchronistic phenomenon, with its curious merging of time, space, image, and object, something of the original transcendental unity becomes visible and can be experienced; and this inrush of the transcendental evokes wonder and fear. It is a natural paradox, for in it the entities merged together in that unitary background reality are not completely separated, not yet completely split apart into the isolation of our time and our space. On the contrary, the psychic and the physical speak the same language: they express the otherwise unknowable archetype, and what binds them together is "a meaning which is *a priori* in relation to human consciousness and apparently exists outside man,"[76] or, in a wider sense, "a modality without a cause, an 'acausal orderedness.' "[77]

The fact that synchronistic events are closely linked with the unconscious, and more specifically with the archetype, explains their unpredictable nature. The contents of the unconscious function autonomously. This is one of the most important discoveries made by analytical psychology in recent decades. The autonomy of unconscious contents gives all manifestations of the unconscious, including extrasensory perceptions, their sporadic and irregular character. Regularity and predictability of events are guaranteed only where the con-

75. *Mysterium Coniunctionis* (CW, 14), par. 769.
76. "Synchronicity," par. 942.
77. *Ibid.*, par. 965.

cepts of space, time, and causality have absolute validity. But this, as we pointed out at the start, is no more the case in the border area between conscious and unconscious than it is in the realm of subatomic or cosmic magnitudes. By their nonconformity with the law of causality, synchronistic phenomena remain irregular, unpredictable events. Jung's initial view was that they are always exceptions. The results of Rhine's experiments, however, modified this view in the sense that they may be expected to occur with some degree of statistical probability. In the same way, as a result of observations of atomic behavior, statistical probability took the place of strict determinism.

Synchronistic phenomena point to the existence of that acausal orderedness we have spoken of, to which both the observing psyche and the observed physical process are subject. The conception of an order anchored in the metaphysical realm places synchronicity, as a principle of cognition, within the framework of conformity to law that runs through the natural sciences; it is only a special instance, widely postulated today, of a transcendental order embracing the worlds within and without, spirit and cosmos. In Jung's own words: "I incline in fact to the view that synchronicity in the narrower sense is only a special instance of general acausal orderedness—that, namely, of the equivalence of psychic and physical processes."[78] One aspect of this orderedness is Jung's postulate of an *absolute knowledge in the unconscious*, or "an 'immediacy' of events which lacks any causal basis."[79] He defined it as "an *a priori*, causally inexplicable knowledge of a situation which at the time is unknowable."[80] An example of this would be Swedenborg's vision of the fire in Stockholm. Another aspect is the hypothesis of an a priori, self-subsistent meaning

78. *Ibid.*
79. *Ibid.*, par. 856; *cf.* also pars. 912, 931.
80. *Ibid.*, par. 858.

to which we referred earlier. But this hypothesis is outside the realm of scientific verification. Nevertheless, the idea of an objective, transcendental meaning allows us to glimpse the numinosity and metaphysical nature of the cosmic order in the background.

It was an important event in the history of science when the explanatory principle of synchronicity raised a bridge between physics and psychology. They meet in the postulate of that a priori orderedness embracing both matter and psyche, and in their acausal connections. Wolfgang Pauli writes:

> Although in physics there is no talk of "self-reproducing archetypes" but of "statistical natural laws with primary probabilities," both formulations meet in the tendency to expand the old, narrower idea of "causality" (determinism) into a more general form of "connections" in nature. The psychophysical problem (i.e., of synchronistic phenomena) also points in this direction. This approach permits me to expect that the concepts of the unconscious will not go on developing within the narrow frame of their therapeutic applications, but that their merging with the general current of science in investigating the phenomena of life is of paramount importance for them.[81]

Physics and psychology have pushed forward into a region that eludes direct observation. An intrinsically unknowable autonomous order must be predicated behind physical phenomena; the corresponding reality behind psychic phenomena is the collective unconscious with its intrinsically unknowable ordering factors, the archetypes. Jung surmised that the

81. Pauli, "Naturwissenschaftliche und erkenntnistheoretische Aspekte der Ideen vom Unbewussten," *Dialectica*, pp. 300–1. Compare this statement with Jung's: "Sooner or later nuclear physics and the psychology of the unconscious will draw closer together as both of them, independently of one another and from opposite directions, push forward into transcendental territory, the one with the concept of the atom, the other with that of the archetype." *Aion* (CW, 9,Part II), par. 412.

two background realities were possibly one and the same entity: "Since psyche and matter are contained in one and the same world, and moreover are in continuous contact with one another and ultimately rest on irrepresentable, transcendental factors, it is not only possible but fairly probable, even, that psyche and matter are two different aspects of one and the same thing."[82]

Synchronistic phenomena point to the psychophysical unity of the transcendental background and carry its paradoxical nature out of that inapprehensible realm into the realm of consciousness. They call for the construction of a new and more complete world model, in which acausal as well as causal connections are acknowledged as real.

> The causalism that underlies our scientific picture of the world breaks everything down into individual processes which it punctiliously tries to isolate from all other parallel processes. This tendency is absolutely necessary if we are to gain a reliable knowledge of the world, but philosophically it has the disadvantage of breaking up, or obscuring, the universal interrelationship of events so that a recognition of the greater relationship, i.e., the unity of the world, becomes more and more difficult. Everything that happens, however, happens in the same "one world" and is part of it. For this reason events must have an *a priori* aspect of unity.[83]

The transcendental, psychoid archetype with its autonomous "arrangements" in the psychic and physical realms allows us to glimpse just that interrelationship of events behind the individual processes. In particular, synchronicity suggests that there is "an interconnection or unity of causally unrelated events, and thus postulates a unitary aspect of being."[84]

82. "On the Nature of the Psyche," *The Structure and Dynamics of the Psyche*, par. 418.
83. *Mysterium Coniunctionis*, par. 662.
84. *Ibid.*

The principle of synchronicity brings the long-lost unity of the world again within the reach of modern thinking, and acts as a compensating element in the disunion and dichotomies of our time. For this reason its significance does not lie only in the realm of psychology and science; it also provides a basis for a new answer to the philosophical question of a world order.

II.

Alchemy

Jung's method of research was pre-eminently historical. It consisted essentially in comparing his ideas and intuitions, and the insights he had gained from the empirical material provided by his patients, with the historical evidence. This method enabled him to view his own psychic experiences and psychological discoveries objectively and to establish their general validity. The obscure, confused, and often grotesque statements of the alchemists played the most important, indeed the decisive, role in this respect. It was largely the correspondence between the alchemical statements and images and the results of his researches into the unconscious that helped Jung to put his psychology into historical perspective and hammer it into an objective science.

During the period of friendship and collaboration with Freud, from 1907 to 1912, Jung had a number of significant dreams which could not be satisfactorily interpreted on the basis of Freud's conception of the unconscious as a reservoir of repressed psychic contents. It was then that the idea of a much more comprehensive unconscious—a *collective* unconscious which was the source of impersonal, autonomous contents—came to him for the first time. After the separation from Freud, Jung followed up this trail and began to experiment with the unconscious himself. He immersed himself in it, using for this purpose a method of "active imagination" which he himself had developed.[1] He would let the contents rise up from the unknown psychic depths, not only carefully observing them but treating them as realities to be lived with, felt, and experienced through active participation. These "imaginings" or fantasies brought up a whole world of strange images, often of a religious or a mythological nature, and he himself became the protagonist in a series of enigmatic but intensely exciting psychic dramas. For the time being, however, the meaning of the images and of what was happening remained for him a complete mystery.

This experimental phase began at the end of 1912 and lasted till about 1919. It was a period of pioneer work in the jungle of the unconscious, which not unnaturally isolated Jung from the scientific world of his time. He nevertheless called those years the most important in his life, for during them there burst forth—if only as a torrent of emotionally charged fantasies and images—everything that was later formulated conceptually in his scientific writings. "It was the *prima materia* for a lifetime's work."[2] The scientific processing of this "fiery magma" was indeed a long-drawn-out affair, and it was only after some twenty years that Jung was able to understand, in some measure, the products of his active imagination.

In his book *Memories, Dreams, Reflections,* he wrote,

> First I had to find evidence for the historical prefiguration of my inner experiences. That is to say, I had to ask myself,

1. *Cf.* "The Transcendent Function," *The Structure and Dynamics of the Psyche* (Collected Works, 8; hereafter CW), pars. 167ff.; *Mysterium Coniunctionis* (CW, 14), pars. 705f, 749, 753ff.; *Analytical Psychology: Its Theory and Practice: The Tavistock Lectures* (London and New York, 1968), pp. 190ff.
2. *Memories, Dreams, Reflections,* recorded and edited by Aniela Jaffé, translated by Richard and Clara Winston (New York and London, 1963), p. 199.

> "Where have my particular premises already occurred in history?" If I had not succeeded in finding such evidence, I would never have been able to substantiate my ideas. Therefore, my encounter with alchemy was decisive for me, as it provided me with the historical basis which I had hitherto lacked.[3]

All the same, a good while had still to pass before Jung became seriously interested in alchemy. Before a lucky chance first brought him face to face with an alchemical text, he had made a thorough study of the Gnostics during the years 1916–26. What attracted him to them was the fact that they had been confronted with "the primal world of the unconscious."[4] just as he and, as he was to discover, the alchemists had been. The study of Gnostic traditions nevertheless left him unsatisfied. For one thing, they were not less than seventeen or eighteen hundred years old and too remote historically for him to establish a living link with them. For another, the tradition that might have connected the Gnostics with the present seemed to him to have been broken. Later Jung realized that alchemy should in fact be considered the connecting link between Gnosticism and the modern psychology of the unconscious. This crucial discovery revealed the unbroken historical continuity of a cultural current that for much of its course flowed underground. There was a continuous chain of great wise men, known in alchemy as the "Golden" or "Homeric Chain," who from antiquity had undertaken the "unpopular, ambiguous, and dangerous voyage of discovery to the other pole of the world,"[5] or, in psychological terms, who had sought to explore the mystery of the psychic hinterland and to bridge the gulf between the conscious and the unconscious.

3. *Ibid.*, p. 200.
4. *Ibid.*, p. 200.
5. *Ibid.*, p. 189.

In 1928 Jung began to study alchemy. Concurrently with his practice, his scientific researches, and the major works he had written in the meantime,[6] the work on his own unconscious had quietly been going ahead. His most important discovery during these years of experimentation was the fact that a process of development was going on in the unconscious which had as its goal the wholeness of the personality. This process (Jung later called it the "individuation" process) frequently depicts itself in the form of images from the unconscious representing the circumambulation of a center. Also the goal of the process, man's psychic totality or the "self," embracing both conscious and unconscious, often appears as a circle, a static mandala. Although he recognized the significance of these figures, for many years Jung kept quiet about the insights he had gained from the practice of active imagination, as well as from the material presented by patients, concerning the meaning of the mandala in relation to the individuation process. The results of his investigations seemed questionable to him in more than one respect. "My results, based on fifteen years of effort, seemed inconclusive, because no possibility of comparison offered itself. I knew of no realm of human experience with which I might have backed up my findings with some degree of assurance."[7]

The turning point came when the Sinologist Richard Wilhelm sent him the manuscript of his translation of a Chinese alchemical treatise of Taoist origin entitled *The Secret of the Golden Flower*,[8] with the request that he write a commentary

6. "La Structure de l'inconscient" (1916) and *Die Psychologie der unbewussten Prozesse* (1917), revised and expanded versions now in *Two Essays on Analytical Psychology* (CW, 7; see also Appendices); *Psychological Types* (1921).

7. Foreword to 2nd German ed. (1938) of *The Secret of the Golden Flower. Cf.* revised English ed. translated by Cary F. Baynes (New York, 1962), p. xiii. Also *Alchemical Studies* (CW, 13), p. 3.

8. Original German edition, 1929.

on the text.[9] It was a rare work quite unknown in Europe at that time, its content deriving from an ancient Chinese esoteric doctrine. The oral transmission of the text goes back to the Tang dynasty (eighth century) and to the esoteric religion of the Golden Elixir of Life, whose founder is said to have been the famous Taoist adept, Lü Yen, according to folklore one of the "eight immortals." Later the text was circulated in manuscript. The first printing dates from the eighteenth century. In 1920 a thousand copies were reprinted in Peking, together with another treatise, the *Hui Ming Ching* (Book of Consciousness and Life), and distributed to a small circle of readers, among them Richard Wilhelm, who was then a missionary in China.[10]

Jung wrote in his memoirs,

> I devoured the manuscript at once, for the text gave me undreamed-of confirmation of my ideas about the mandala and the circumambulation of the centre. That was the first event which broke through my isolation. I became aware of an affinity; I could establish ties with something and someone.[11]

For Jung it was a surprise and a satisfaction to find in this old Chinese alchemical text, based on meditative practices, symbols for psychic contents and psychic states that were well-known to him from personal experience and that of his patients. In the first place he was struck by the mandala symbolism: a most unexpected analogy presented itself between the "circumambulation of the centre" he had discovered and the Chinese concept of the "circulation of the light."[12] Here too the

9. Commentary in *ibid.*, English eds. (1931/1962), and *Alchemical Studies.*

10. *Cf. The Secret of the Golden Flower* (1962), pp. 3ff. References below are to this edition.

11. *Memories, Dreams, Reflections*, p. 197.

12. *Golden Flower*, pp. 30–53; *Alchemical Studies*, pars. 31ff.

circular movement was intended to set in motion a development of personality leading to individuation. The visionary golden flower or flower of light which the circulation causes to blossom forth in the center of this movement is a true mandala symbol. Psychologically, it is a symbol of the self.

A further analogy is to be found in the two concepts for the soul, personified by the masculine "cloud demon" *hun* and the feminine, earthbound "white ghost" *p'o*, which Jung interpreted as equivalents of the animus and anima.[13] Above all, there was an affinity between the goals to be reached: the production of the "diamond body"[14] through meditation was a symbol for the shifting of the psychic center from the ego to a transpersonal, spiritual authority. The meditative process thus involved a psychic transformation which Jung had recognized and experienced as the goal of individuation: the recession of the ego in favor of the totality of the self. Nothing less than this was also sought by the Western adepts of the hermetic art in their endeavors to produce the incorruptible stone, the *lapis philosophorum.*

The affinity of images and ideas which emerged from the meditations of Western and Chinese practitioners alike brought Jung the long awaited confirmation of his conception of the collective unconscious and also of the archetypes. The presence of these organizing factors and structural forms in the unconscious would explain the similarity and sometimes even the identity of myth-motifs and symbols found among all races and in all parts of the world. Jung called such images and motifs "archetypal." Their practical importance lies not least in the fact that they facilitate human communication in general, and indeed make it possible at all. Recognition of the common archetypal contents and motifs behind the differences

13. *Golden Flower,* pp. 115ff., see also pp. 14–15; *Alchemical Studies,* pars. 57ff.

14. *Golden Flower,* p. 98; *Alchemical Studies,* pars. 28–29.

between individuals and cultures helps them to understand what is alien to them. Jung described his commentary on *The Secret of the Golden Flower* as an "attempt to build a bridge of psychological understanding between East and West."[15]

Richard Wilhelm, too, was surprised and impressed by the similarities between Jung's findings and ancient Chinese wisdom. He expressed his astonishment by saying that he had "encountered Jung in China." He went on,

> Chinese wisdom and Dr. Jung have both descended independently of one another into the depths of man's collective psyche and have there come upon realities which look so alike because they are equally anchored in the truth. This would prove that the truth can be reached from any standpoint if only one digs deep enough for it, and the congruity between the Swiss scientist and the old Chinese sages only goes to show that both are right because both have found the truth.[16]

Even so, Jung never failed to stress the other aspect of the human personality: the common archetypal foundation of the psyche can become a meaningful reality only in the diversity of individual lives, variously conditioned as they are by history, culture, tradition, and by constitution and environment. The psychic background—the collective unconscious and the archetypes—is everywhere the same; the conscious configuration in the foreground is always unique, combining and varying the archetypal figures in ways that are ever new.

The Secret of the Golden Flower had thoroughly aroused Jung's interest in alchemy. Soon afterwards he acquired the first alchemical work for his library from a bookseller in Munich. It was the two volumes of *Artis Auriferae*, a compilation of some thirty Latin treatises, published in Basel in 1593.

15. *Golden Flower*, p. 136; *Alchemical Studies*, par. 83.
16. Wilhelm, "Meine Begegnung mit C. G. Jung in China," *Neue Zürcher Zeitung*, 21 January 1929.

This did not remain his only acquisition, for he soon turned into a collector, and in the course of the years his alchemical books and manuscripts came to constitute a substantial part of his library. After his death, over two hundred items were catalogued.

Important events in Jung's life often announced themselves beforehand in dreams. Such was the case with his discovery of alchemy. Jung tells about it in his memoirs:

> Before I discovered alchemy, I had a series of dreams which repeatedly dealt with the same theme. Beside my house stood another, that is to say, another wing or annex, which was strange to me. Each time I would wonder in my dream why I did not know this house, although it had apparently always been there. Finally came a dream in which I reached the other wing. I discovered there a wonderful library, dating largely from the sixteenth and seventeenth centuries. Large, fat folio volumes, bound in pigskin, stood along the walls. Among them were a number of books embellished with copper engravings of a strange character, and illustrations containing curious symbols such as I had never seen before. At the time I did not know to what they referred; only much later did I recognize them as alchemical symbols. In the dream I was conscious only of the fascination exerted by them and by the entire library. It was a collection of medieval incunabula and sixteenth-century printings.
>
> The unknown wing of the house . . . and especially the library, referred to alchemy, of which I was ignorant, but which I was soon to study. Some fifteen years later I had assembled a library very like the one in the dream.[17]

The dream goes back to about the year 1925. In 1940 Jung's collection was more or less completed. He was well aware of its value and its rarity, and this was a source of pleasure to him. With true collector's pride he would show his library to book-lovers whenever opportunity offered. Yet he was no biblio-

17. *Memories, Dreams, Reflections,* p. 202.

phile in the ordinary sense of the word. He collected books not for their own sake but for their content. Among them were photocopies of two alchemical manuscripts, the *Codex Vossianus Chemicus*[18] from the University of Leiden, and the eighteenth-century *Livre des figures hiéroglifiques* of Abraham le Juif[19] from the Bibliothèque Nationale, Paris, as well as modern works like the three volumes of Marcellin Berthelot's *Collection des anciens alchimistes grecs* (Paris, 1893).

In the course of his psychological interpretation of alchemical texts, which were then not understood at all, Jung came to realize the truth of the alchemical saying "liber librum aperit" (one book opens another). For this reason he wanted to study the texts in their entirety and, if possible, to own them.

Jung's collection still stands today in the spacious study-*cum*-library, unchanged since his death, in his house in Küsnacht, a suburb of Zurich.[20] The library is open to students, but the alchemical collection, because of its rarity, is to be used only by specially qualified persons.

Fundamentally it was not the thoughts of individual alchemists that were of importance for Jung's researches so much as the inexhaustible variety of their arcane images and descriptions, apparently so different yet all interrelated. In this sense his collection was an indispensable help to him and a mine of psychological insights. There was no particular book that he

18. For illustrations from this Codex, see *Psychology and Alchemy* (CW, 12), Figs. 9, 17, 20, 38, 90, 99, 129, 140, 152, 201, 241.

19. *Ibid.*, Fig. 217.

20. In this room is his writing desk, and here he used to receive patients and friends. A window and a glass door opening on to a narrow balcony face southeast and look out across the garden and the lake towards the mountains. On clear days the afternoon sun floods through the room. The alchemical books are ranged on the wall between the window and the glass door, protected from sun and light. A large, handsome old stove of green tiles stands beside another door leading to a second, smaller library. Today the house is occupied by Jung's son, the architect Franz Jung, and his family.

valued above all others. He would single out one or another according to its applicability to the theme he was interested in and was writing about at the moment. In his old age Gerard Dorn, a learned natural philosopher, doctor, and Paracelsist from Frankfurt-am-Main, who lived in the sixteenth century, came to mean more to Jung than most other alchemists. Dorn's profound meditations on the spiritual significance of the alchemical opus, on the three stages of the *coniunctio*, and on the concept of the *unus mundus* (unitary world) gave him a clue to the meaning of the alchemists' labors and are discussed in great detail in the last chapter of his *Mysterium Coniunctionis.* One of the books most frequently quoted by Jung is the anonymous *Rosarium philosophorum;* it was first published in Frankfurt in 1550,[21] and is also contained in the second volume of *Artis Auriferae.* Jung's monograph "The Psychology of the Transference"[22] is a detailed interpretation of the text and illustrations of this treatise.

At one of my first analytical sessions during the late thirties Jung greeted me with the words that he wanted to show me something "very precious and secret." He fetched a slim folio volume down from the shelves and gave it to me. It was called *Mutus Liber,* a picture book with no text,[23] published in La Rochelle in 1677, the first alchemical book I ever held in my hands. Looking at its pictures and talking about alchemy, we passed one of those unconventional analytical hours which were characteristic of Jung's "method" and exerted a lasting influence.

In his memoirs Jung tells us something about the method which gave him a key to the language of alchemy, its obscurities and riddles.

21. It forms the second volume of *De Alchimia opuscula complura.*
22. Contained in *The Practice of Psychotherapy* (CW, 16).
23. For illustrations see *Psychology and Alchemy,* Figs. 2, 22, 113, 124, 132, 133, 143, 161, 215, 237, 269.

> It was a long while before I found my way about in the labyrinth of alchemical thought processes, for no Ariadne had put a thread into my hand. Reading the sixteenth-century text, *Rosarium philosophorum,* I noticed that certain strange expressions and turns of phrase were frequently repeated. For example, "solve et coagula," "unum vas," "lapis," "prima materia," "Mercurius," etc. I saw that these expressions were used again and again in a particular sense, but I could not make out what that sense was. I therefore decided to start a lexicon of key phrases with cross references. In the course of time I assembled several thousand such key phrases and words, and had volumes filled with excerpts. I worked along philological lines, as if I were trying to solve the riddle of an unknown language. In this way the alchemical mode of expression gradually yielded up its meaning. It was a task that kept me absorbed for more than a decade.[24]

In 1935, after years of alchemical study, Jung presented his findings to the public for the first time. At the Eranos meeting in Ascona, Switzerland, he gave a lecture entitled "Dream Symbols of the Individuation Process," which traced the alchemical parallels in the dreams of a modern individual, and the following year he lectured on "The Idea of Redemption in Alchemy."[25] During seven more years of intensive research these lectures were elaborated into one of his key works, *Psychology and Alchemy* (originally published in 1944). The Eranos lectures had already made it clear why the alchemical texts were so important as sources for investigating the unconscious: the alchemical opus could not be regarded as a purely chemical procedure. To a far higher degree than was generally recognized, it was psychic in origin.[26]

Matter, for the alchemists, was still a mystery. It is a psycho-

24. *Memories, Dreams, Reflections,* p. 205.

25. *Eranos Jahrbuch 1935* and *1936* (Zurich, 1936 and 1937).

26. Before Jung, Herbert Silberer had discussed the psychological aspects of alchemy in his book *Problems of Mysticism and Its Symbolism* (orig. Vienna, 1914; translated by Smith Ely Jelliffe, New York, 1917).

logical rule that the unconscious is constellated whenever a person is confronted with something unknown. New psychic contents rise up in the form of images and get mixed with the unknown object, seeming to make it come alive and intelligible. This was what happened to the alchemists. What they experienced as properties of matter was in reality the content of their own unconscious, and the psychic experiences they had while working in their laboratories appeared to them as the peculiar transformations of chemical substances. Although, as Jung says, the adept's preoccupation with matter may be regarded as a "serious effort to elicit the secrets of chemical transformation, it was at the same time—and often in overwhelming degree—the reflection of a parallel psychic process."[27] Thus it came about that the alchemist projected another mystery into the mystery he was trying to explain; namely, his own unknown psychic background. In the alchemical symbolism, the stages and imagery of an inner process of transformation were expressing themselves in pseudochemical language. "Consequently alchemy gains the quite new and interesting aspect of a *projected psychology of the collective unconscious*, and thus ranks with mythology and folklore. Its symbolism is in the closest relation to dream symbolism on the one hand, and to the symbolism of religion on the other."[28]

Naturally Jung was eager to find texts that would bear out the nonchemical nature of the complicated alchemical procedures, showing that though the old masters busied themselves with alembics and furnaces in the attempt to produce the metallic gold, they were also aware of the psychic background and the deeper, religious significance of the transformation

27. *Psychology and Alchemy*, par. 40.

28. Jung, preface (written in English) to a catalogue of alchemical books issued by the antiquarian bookseller K. A. Ziegler, Zurich. Reprinted in *Alchemy and the Occult*, A Catalogue of Books and Manuscripts from the Collection of Paul and Mary Mellon (Yale University Library, 1968), Vol. I, p. vii.

processes they described. This he soon succeeded in doing. In the oldest as well as the more recent texts he came upon hints as to the psychic aspect of these procedures, and found descriptions of the dreamlike, visionary experiences that often accompanied the opus. The *Book of Krates* (ninth century)[29] presents the whole alchemical doctrine in the form of a dream. In a late treatise by Abtala Jurain, alleged to have been translated from Ethiopian into Latin and from Latin into German,[30] the author describes how, on letting a few drops of the "consecrated red wine" fall into a vessel of carefully prepared and clarified rainwater, the story of the creation of the world was re-enacted before his eyes, "how it all came to pass, and such secrets as are not to be spoken aloud and I also have not the power to reveal."[31] "Seeing with the eyes of the spirit or the understanding" is a phrase used by several authors, among them Michael Sendivogius (seventeenth century) in his treatise "Novum lumen": "To cause things hidden in the shadow to appear, and to take away the shadow from them, this is permitted to the intelligent philosopher by God through nature. . . . All these things happen, and the eyes of the common men do not see them, but the eyes of the understanding and of the imagination perceive them with true and truest vision."[32] In sayings like "aurum nostrum non est aurum vulgi" (our gold is not the common gold), and in the concepts "lapis invisibilitatis," "lapis philosophorum," "lapis aethereus," "lapis est spiritus," and the axiom "tam ethice quam physice" (as much ethical–i.e., psychic–as physical), as well as countless other metaphors in the same vein, the spiritual side of

29. In Berthelot, *La Chimie au moyen-âge* (Paris, 1893), Vol. III, pp. 44ff. See also *Psychology and Alchemy*, par. 349, n. 7.

30. The full title is *Abtala Jurain Filii Jacob Juran, Hyle und Coahyl, aus dem Aethiopischen ins Lateinische, und aus dem Lateinischen in das Teutsche übersetzt von Johann Elias Müller* (Hamburg, 1732).

31. *Psychology and Alchemy*, par. 347.

32. *Ibid.*, par. 350, from the *Musaeum Hermeticum* (Frankfort, 1678), p. 574.

alchemy is revealed in all clarity. Above all, the ever repeated attempts to describe the enigmatic qualities and transformations of matter contain such a wealth of religious ideas, so many allusions to a hidden numen, that they endow alchemy with the significance of a *religious movement.* It was this aspect that gripped Jung's interest. For him the psyche was "one of the darkest and most mysterious regions of our experience,"[33] and the greatest of all its mysteries was the genesis of religious symbols. This mystery came to light in alchemical projections, in the meditations and visions of the adept.

Matter for the alchemists was a source of numinosity. They saw it as the vessel of a captive, divine spirit from which it had to be liberated. For the Paracelsists, matter acquired the ineffable quality of an "increatum," and hence was coexistent and coeternal with God.[34] Since it was conceived as a spiritual and even divine substance, it is hardly surprising that the alchemist's experimental work in the laboratory, his philosophizing, his dreamlike immersion in its transformations, and the practical investigation of its qualities took on the character of a religious rite, an *opus divinum.* Jung's "Introduction to the Religious and Psychological Problems of Alchemy"[35] is one of his most important contributions to the creativity and religious nature of the psyche.

The theme "anima naturaliter religiosa" (the soul is by nature religious) was one that engrossed Jung for the greater part of his life. In "Psychology and Religion"[36] (the Terry Lectures, delivered at Yale University in 1937), he developed this theme on the basis of his 1935 Eranos lecture. His point of departure was a comparison of archetypal motifs–mandala,

33. *Ibid.*, par. 2.
34. *Mysterium Coniunctionis*, par. 766.
35. *Psychology and Alchemy*, Part I.
36. In *Psychology and Religion: West and East* (CW, 11).

circle divided into four, quaternity—such as are common in alchemical literature, with the dreams of a modern man who had no knowledge of alchemy.[37] They were significant, "big" dreams of an unquestionably religious character, one of which left behind on the dreamer an impression of "most sublime harmony."[38] For the alchemists such symbols and configurations were no less impressive, no less rich in secret meanings. In particular it was the *rotundum* or sphere that was considered a symbol of the supreme religious or spiritual reality in both old and late texts, thus bearing out Jung's discovery of the mandala symbol and its meaning: in Western as well as Eastern alchemy the circle must be regarded as one of the central archetypal figures of the collective unconscious. For the alchemists it was identical with the incorruptible philosophers' stone, and it also signified the sought-for gold; in either form it referred to the "treasure hard to attain" and the goal that had to be reached "tam ethice quam physice." Combined with the quaternity as a circle divided into four, or as the famous squaring of the circle, it was counted an allegory of God. It seems surprising at first that a symbol with such profound religious implications should have its place in alchemical speculation. But it is so only if alchemy is understood as pseudo chemistry and the labors of the adepts as an expression of genuine religious aspiration are overlooked. Their mysticism of matter was fundamentally a mysticism of the soul; psychologically speaking, they were gripped by the numinous images and symbols of the unconscious which they beheld in the medium of matter.

It was only natural that in their attempts to describe the properties, behavior, and transformations of chemical sub-

37. The dreams here discussed were taken from the series later published in *Psychology and Alchemy*, Part II.
38. *Ibid.*, par. 309.

stances, their visionary experiences and religious intuitions should also have been alluded to symbolically. This accounts for the bizarre, grotesque, and sometimes barely decipherable mélange of chemical, philosophical, religious, and profane concepts and images, and for the scurrilous language of some alchemical texts. Equally scurrilous and fantastic are the woodcuts and colored vignettes that adorn the old works and often make a powerful impact. It was a style that found its way into profane art and reached a high pitch of perfection in Hieronymus Bosch.

The profusion of paradoxes which is characteristic of alchemical language can be explained by the fact that the adepts were seeking to express unconscious contents only dimly discerned or experienced as in a dream. Clear statements are possible only in an area illuminated by consciousness, *i.e.*, about concepts and facts that can be elucidated by rational thought. What transcends consciousness, what falls within the realm of the unconscious, can be adequately described only by paradoxes. "Unequivocal statements can be made only in regard to immanent objects; transcendental ones can be expressed only by paradox," says Jung.[39] Through imagination and speculation the old masters were endeavoring to find or to produce a matter that was not only matter but also spirit. They called it the "arcane substance," and they sought to grasp it by an infinity of paradoxes and antinomies. Jung's interpretive comparisons have shown it to be a symbol of the unconscious.

Although the majority of the alchemists considered themselves good Christians, according to some of them the "mystery of the stone" was even more sublime than the mystery of the Christian religion. Melchior Cibinensis (sixteenth century)

39. *Mysterium Coniunctionis*, par. 715.

represented the alchemical opus as a paraphrase of the Mass,[40] and for Paracelsus, who in this proved himself a true alchemist, there was a revelation "from the light of nature" which was equal to the Christian revelation.[41] A magnificent example of the religious character of alchemy in relation to the Bible and Christianity is the first part of *Aurora Consurgens,* a treatise attributed to Thomas Aquinas.[42] The compilation *Artis Auriferae* contains only the second part, and in place of the first there is an instructive notice, written in Latin by the typographer, in which he explains and justifies his refusal to print it on religious grounds. Jung gives a précis of the argument in *Psychology and Alchemy.*

> He [the printer] has purposely omitted the entire treatise consisting of parables or allegories because the author, in the manner of obscurantists (*antiquo more tenebrionum*), treated almost the whole Bible—particularly Proverbs, Psalms, but above all the Song of Songs—in such a way as to suggest that the Holy Scripture had been written solely in honour of alchemy. The author, he says, has even profaned the most holy mystery of the incarnation and death of Christ by turning it into the mystery of the *lapis*—not, of course, with any evil intent, as he, the typographer Conrad Waldkirch, readily admits, but as was only to be expected in that benighted epoch (*seculum illud tenebrarum*). By this Waldkirch meant the

40. "Addam et processum sub forma missae," in *Theatrum Chemicum,* Vol. III (1602), pp. 853ff. For a summary, see *Psychology and Alchemy,* pars. 480ff.

41. *Cf.* "Paracelsus as a Spiritual Phenomenon," *Alchemical Studies,* pars. 148–50.

42. Several manuscripts in various states of preservation exist, and there is a printing in Johannes Rhenanus, *Harmoniae inperscrutabilis chymico-philosophicae Decades duae* (Frankfort, 1625). The text of *Aurora* has been translated into German, with commentary, by M.-L. von Franz, as a companion volume to Jung's *Mysterium Coniunctionis.* An English translation entitled *Aurora Consurgens: A Document Attributed to Thomas Aquinas on the Problem of Opposites in Alchemy* was published in Bollingen Series, Vol. LXXVII (New York, 1966). Concerning the manuscripts, see pp. 25ff.

> pre-Reformation epoch, whose conception of man and the world, and experience of the divine presence in the mystery of matter, had entirely vanished from the purview of the Protestants of his own day.[43]

The image of God or of spirit which was central to the alchemical mystery was by no means identical with the supreme conception of God in Christianity. From the numerical standpoint they differ in that the alchemical conception is characterized by the quaternity—in keeping with the Gnostic saying "In the Four is God"[44]—whereas the Christian conception found its most differentiated expression in the Holy Trinity. Alchemical speculations concerning the mystery gravitate round the idea of a spirit which manifests itself in the whole of Creation, in matter as well as in man—an "anima media natura" (soul as intermediate nature), likewise of Gnostic origin, an image which goes back to the ancient myth of Nous locked in the embrace of Physis.[45]

Because of its elusive nature, this spirit or "divine presence in the mystery of matter" was named Mercurius. Other names were *filius macrocosmi*, *salvator*, *elixir vitae*, *deus terrenus*, and *lapis*—in so far as the latter was understood to be spirit. The spirit of the alchemical mystery was a chthonic spirit, and unlike the masculine Trinity it did not lack the feminine element. When personified in the alchemical illustrations, it was for this reason usually represented as androgynous.[46] There are also hints that it contained the element of darkness and evil. In contrast to the unequivocal meaning of the Son in Christianity, the alchemical *filius* was the subject of innumerable paradoxes and was described as the son of Mother Nature.

43. Par. 464.
44. *Cf.* H. Leisegang, "Die Barbelo-Gnostiker," *Die Gnosis* (Leipzig, 1924), pp. 186ff.
45. *Cf. Psychology and Alchemy*, par. 410.
46. *Ibid.*, Fig. 125.

Alchemy thus stood in a compensatory relationship to the world of consciousness and to Christianity, just as a dream does to the conscious situation of the dreamer. Compounded of the natural and often primitive manifestations of the unconscious, it reflected the lofty, spiritual concepts of Christian dogma as in a dark mirror. Moreover, its images, having their origin in the earlier and deeper layers of the psyche, contain numerous archetypal and numinous elements that were eliminated from dogmatic theology.

The compensatory relationship between alchemical and Christian imagery gave Jung the Ariadne thread by which he found his way through the labyrinth of hermetic literature and the archetypal world of the psychic hinterland. In a number of essays he pointed out the affinities and contrasts between the alchemical figures and those of Christianity, demonstrating in particular the strange, mirror-like analogy between the statements about the *lapis* and Christ. The *lapis* too was a redeemer, a "savior of the macrocosm"; its light conquered all lights, it was spirit and body, the stone which the builders rejected and became the cornerstone, but it was also a *deus terrenus*, an earth god, the begetter not only of light but of darkness. "The Lapis-Christ Parallel" in *Psychology and Alchemy* provides a clue to an understanding of the piety of the alchemists and its relation to Christianity. Elsewhere Jung contrasted the transformation in the Mass with an analogous transformation process described in the visions of Zosimos of Panopolis, an alchemist of the third century,[47] and compared the Christian ideas of redemption with those of the alchemists.[48]

In the alchemical opus it is not man who is in need of redemption but matter, or rather, the spirit imprisoned in matter, in the darkness of physical nature. The adept himself

47. "Transformation Symbolism in the Mass," *Psychology and Religion: West and East*, and "The Visions of Zosimos," *Alchemical Studies*.
48. *Cf. Psychology and Alchemy*, Part III, chaps. 3 and 4.

undertook the task of redeeming the chaotic *prima materia*, accomplishing the work of redemption, stage by stage, as his own individual opus.[49] From the psychological point of view this work was a projection of the individuation process into the transformations of the chemical substance. Like the alchemical opus, individuation is a wearisome procedure to be accomplished in stages: by consciously collaborating with the unconscious, the individuant performs a work of self-redemption that makes him a whole and undivided personality, an "individual." The production of the alchemical "treasure" corresponds to the deliverance, or bringing-to-consciousness, of the self from the darkness and primal chaos of the unconscious.

It took many centuries before man's consciousness was sufficiently developed to withdraw the alchemical projections into matter and to recognize as psychic that which had been psychic from the very beginning. It is one of the outstanding achievements of Jung's scientific work that it contributed toward this mental revolution. The conceptual distinction between projection and object, or image and object, was for him an epistemological necessity of universal validity which he demanded of every science. At the same time, it was the study of alchemical projections that enabled him to embark on a wholly new investigation of the archetypal contents of the collective unconscious and to view his own work in the light of a process of human development extending over thousands of years. By comparing the contents of the unconscious in modern man with those of alchemy (whose historical roots go back to Egyptian mythology), he came to see that archetypal images portray the basic facts of the psyche which have remained the same for thousands of years and will remain the same for thousands more. Only in their relationship to the conscious mind can we discern an infinitely slow development,

49. *Ibid.*, pars. 414ff.

pursuing its course like a "drama that began in the grey mists of antiquity and continues through the centuries into a remote future—a drama that makes the present seem but an episode. This drama is . . . the dawning of consciousness in mankind."[50]

The results of his researches not only led to differentiations of theory within psychology itself but also afforded a deeper understanding of the problems that arise in practical psychotherapy. As a doctor, Jung was daily confronted with the still-unresolved problem of assimilating the "darkness" and "evil" in human nature, which had a perfectly natural place in alchemy and was expressed in the symbolism of the dragon, unicorn, serpent, *nigredo*, quaternity, etc. He became passionately interested in this question, because for him it was not only a religious and moral problem but the eminently practical one of assimilating the "shadow"—the inferior side of the personality. His observations on the religious aspect of evil start from the ancient numerical dilemma that runs through alchemy: the opposition and interplay of the trinity and the quaternity, where the "fourth" takes over the role of evil.[51] The definitive formulation of this theme is to be found in "Answer to Job."[52]

Another practical problem which Jung reinterpreted in a deeper sense on the basis of alchemy was the process which Freud called the "transference." Both Freud and Jung attributed a crucial role to this psychotherapeutic phenomenon. Jung chose the alchemical illustrations in the *Rosarium philosophorum* as a starting point for his exposition of the problem of interpersonal and psychic relationships in the aforementioned monograph, "The Psychology of the Transference."

50. *Ibid.*, par. 556.

51. *Cf.* "A Psychological Approach to the Dogma of the Trinity," *Psychology and Religion: West and East*, esp. Chap. 5, and *Aion* (CW, 9, Part II), esp. Chap. V.

52. In *Psychology and Religion: West and East.*

Although the peculiar and sometimes scurrilous pictures in the *Rosarium* are not conscious representations of the transference phenomenon, they portray it as the unconscious premise underlying erotic relationships in general. Jung compared the various "stages of conjunction" they depict with the stages of the transference and the transformations it brings about, which in turn may be regarded as the stages and transformations of the individuation process.

If any work of Jung's is calculated to refute the exclusively personalistic and sexual interpretation of human relationships, it is this monograph. Behind the bond between the sexes stands the self, the archetype of wholeness, which contains and at the same time unites the opposites in human nature. This duality and unity are expressed in the figurative language of alchemy by pairs of opposites such as Rex and Regina, Adam and Eve, Sol and Luna, bird and snake, or by the more general and abstract concept of a *coincidentia oppositorum.* In the world of consciousness the transpersonal, paradoxical unity of the self, the alchemical conjunction of sun and moon, is experienced as a synthesis of "I and Thou." In so far as "Thou" is projected upon (*i.e.*, transferred to) another person–in psychotherapeutic treatment, the analyst–the transference relationship at least gives the patient an anticipatory experience of wholeness and the possibility of realizing it by withdrawing the projection. The stages of the transference thus become a way of psychic development and so create the basis for a cure. "The conventional guises are dropped and the true man comes to light. He is in very truth reborn from this psychological relationship."[53] The progressive realization of the self and a consideration of those aspects of wholeness which come to consciousness through fantasies and through the variegated facets of the transference raise the interhuman relationship out

53. "The Psychology of the Transference," *The Practice of Psychotherapy*, par. 420.

of the realm of personal entanglements and set it in the wider context of a transpersonal, psychic process with subtle shades of meaning that can be properly expressed only in symbols. Among the alchemists also there were some who did not work alone, but sought the gold or the mysterious stone with the help of a female companion, the *soror mystica.* The gold and the stone signified wholeness.

Variations on the transference theme occur in the symbols of the "chymical wedding," the *unio mystica,* and the immense field of traditional *hierosgamos* symbolism. This reaches all the way from ancient Egypt to the Helen episode in the second part of *Faust,* and is still alive today not only in the unconscious of modern man–as is evidenced by dreams, visions, and artistic creations–but, surprisingly enough, in Christian dogma as well. The dogma of the Assumption of the Virgin Mary, promulgated by Pope Pius XII in 1950, contains several allusions to the "heavenly marriage,"[54] thus proving how the unconscious world of images reasserts its timeless significance as a dark counterpart to the spiritual world of Christianity. Both are concerned with the *mysterium coniunctionis.*

The central alchemical image for the polarity of the psyche is Mercurius, whose extraordinary diversity of meanings Jung has discussed in a special study.[55] As "Mercurius duplex" and *utriusque capax* (capable of both), he is the source of all opposites, for which reason the alchemists endowed him with a bewildering variety of names and paradoxical qualities. "He is God, daemon, person, thing, and the innermost secret in

54. *Apostolic Constitution* ("*Munificentissimus Deus*") *of . . . Pius XII,* sect. 22: "The place of the bride whom the Father had espoused was in the heavenly courts." Sect. 33: ". . . so in like manner arose the Ark which he had sanctified, when on this day the Virgin Mother was taken up to her heavenly bridal-chamber." *Cf.* "Answer to Job" (CW, 11), par. 743, n. 4, and Chap. XIX.

55. "The Spirit Mercurius," *Alchemical Studies.*

man."[56] His polarity is such that he comprises not merely masculine-feminine, good-evil, light-dark, conscious-unconscious, etc.; the paradox of Mercurius is far more profound and even more baffling. He has to be understood as a symbol of the unconscious itself, and his nature expresses the opposites that are inherent within it. In alchemical tradition he is both a material and a spiritual being: quicksilver, and at the same time an elusive spirit of immense power.

This realization brought Jung up against one of the most important and difficult theoretical problems confronting the psychology of the unconscious. He had advanced as a hypothesis a corresponding antinomy regarding the nature of the unconscious or, to be more precise, the nature of the inexperienceable and unknowable (because it is unconscious) archetype per se that underlies the archetypal image.[57] He described it as "psychoid," that is, not purely psychic but to a certain extent physical and organic. One might say that it too is *utriusque capax.*

The hypothesis of a psychoid archetype and a psychoid unconscious proved to have surprising parallels with the findings of microphysics, which in its turn had reached the limits of the experienceable. "Microphysics is feeling its way into the unknown side of matter, just as complex psychology is pushing forward into the unknown side of the psyche,"[58] and microphysics is faced equally with the necessity of hypothesizing this unknown as a psychophysical unity. Wolfgang Pauli has postulated a transcendental and objective "cosmic order" to which both the psyche of "the perceiver and that which is recognized by perception are subject."[59] Inner and

56. "The Philosophical Tree," *ibid.*, par. 481.

57. "On the Nature of the Psyche," *The Structure and Dynamics of the Psyche* (CW, 8), pars. 417ff., 439ff.

58. *Mysterium Coniunctionis*, par. 768.

59. "The Influence of Archetypal Ideas on the Scientific Theories of Kepler," *The Interpretation of Nature and the Psyche* (London and New York, 1955), p. 152.

outer, psychic and physical reality are manifestations of the same structuring order. C. F. von Weizsäcker declares that matter is "in reality only the objectivable manifestation of something else, for which the name chosen by the classical tradition of our philosophy is probably still the best, the name 'spirit.' "[60] Jung for his part conjectured that the "unknown side of matter" and the "unknown side of the psyche" have a common transcendental background, that "in the Unknown beyond our experience" matter and psyche may be identical,[61] and that the whole of life, the multiplicity of our inner and outer world "rests on an underlying unity."[62] This common background is antinomian and must remain inaccessible to investigation. It is "as much physical as psychic and therefore neither, but rather a third thing, a neutral nature which can at most be grasped in hints since in essence it is transcendental.[63] To put it more simply, all reality is "grounded on an as yet unknown substrate possessing material and at the same time psychic qualities."[64] Reverting to this idea of a transcendental unitary reality in his memoirs, Jung admitted that he had "reached the bounds of scientific understanding,"[65] for which reason he called *Mysterium Coniunctionis* the culmination of his work.

The alchemical texts on which Jung based his final summing up were the "Physica Trismegisti" and "Philosophia meditativa" of Gerard Dorn.[66] Dorn used the term *unus mundus* to denote the "third thing," the "neutral" background reality where the unknown in matter and psyche coincide. The *unus*

60. "Gedanken zur Zukunft der Technischen Welt," *Neue Zürcher Zeitung*, 10 October 1967.
61. *Mysterium Coniunctionis*, par. 765.
62. *Ibid.*, par. 767.
63. *Ibid.*, par. 768.
64. "Flying Saucers: A Modern Myth of Things Seen in the Skies," *Civilization in Transition* (CW, 10), par. 780.
65. *Memories, Dreams, Reflections*, p. 221.
66. In *Theatrum Chemicum*, Vol. I (1602), pp. 405ff. and 450ff.

mundus was the unknowable, paradoxical, unitary world beyond the microcosm and macrocosm. If ever the adept succeeded in establishing relations with it, "the consummation of the *mysterium coniunctionis*" would be attained.[67] The mythical, personified image of the third thing with its neutral nature was Mercurius, that mysterious archetypal figure, both divine and psychic, whose ungraspable essence was thought of as both matter and spirit.

By 1952, in his researches into synchronicity, Jung had postulated a transconscious background common to psyche and physis. It was no accident that his essay on synchronicity appeared together with the paper by Wolfgang Pauli.[68] By "synchronistic phenomena" Jung meant the unexpected, meaningful coincidence of a psychic and a physical event which are not causally connected—for instance of a dream or a premonition that comes true and the temporally or spatially distant event it anticipates. The connecting link between these inner and outer events is the equivalence of their content, because of which their coincidence is registered and experienced as meaningful. The equivalence of content in such qualitatively different events, separated in time and space but acausally connected, must be due to the fact that the same archetype in the unconscious underlies both and "arranges" them. It is the unknowable *psychoid* archetype that manifests itself in the world of consciousness, appearing here as a psychic and there as a physical event. The archetype per se belongs to the realm of the collective unconscious, that antinomian world in the background which is "as much physical as psychic and therefore neither. . . ." Consciousness breaks down into separate processes that which is still a unity in the unconscious, thereby dissolving or obscuring the original interrelationship of events

67. *Mysterium Coniunctionis*, par. 767.
68. See p. 69, n. 59 above. Jung's contribution, "Synchronicity: An Acausal Connecting Principle," is republished, with revisions, in *The Structure and Dynamics of the Psyche.*

in the "one world." In Jung's view, synchronistic phenomena, or the acausal correspondences between mutually independent psychic and physical events, necessitate the construction of a new, unitary world-model. The inner and outer worlds of spirit and matter are no longer opposites that cannot be united, but are aspects of that psychoid realm of reality on which they both rest. This new world-model is a reconstruction of the old, intuitive vision of the alchemists; for, as Jung points out, such a model would be "closer to the idea of the *unus mundus*."[69]

Besides the *unus mundus*, there were other alchemical concepts which we have already mentioned—arcane substance, Mercurius, *lapis*—that pointed to a psychophysical unity. So far as the laborant was concerned, one of the most important concepts in this respect was the *imaginatio*, the fantasy activity inseparably connected with the opus. Astonishingly enough, the alchemist conceived his *imaginationes* as something quasi-corporeal, a sort of "subtle body" that was half spiritual. They were, therefore, of a psychoid nature, forming an intermediate realm belonging to both matter and spirit. On account of the mysterious and manifold implications of the *imaginatio*, Jung called it "perhaps the most important key to an understanding of the *opus*."[70]

The "subtle body," or "breath body" as it is sometimes called, is an archetypal idea that can be traced back to classical antiquity. It occurs in Poseidonius and Plotinus, in Proclus and Synesius, and later in Paracelsus.[71] Among the alchemists the idea of a subtle body grew out of their endeavors to find and transform the unknown, arcane substance by means of the

69. "Flying Saucers," par. 780.
70. *Psychology and Alchemy*, par. 396.
71. *Cf.* C. A. Meier, "Psychosomatic Medicine from the Jungian Point of View," *Journal of Analytical Psychology* (London), Vol. 8, No. 2, July 1963, pp. 111–12.

imaginatio. In their projections the psychic and the physical coalesced into a single experience. So it is not surprising that the intermediate realm of subtle bodies disappeared from view after man had freed matter from psychic projections and began investigating it for its own sake, and chemistry and physics had evolved out of alchemy. Equally, the idea of a subtle body was bound to lose its significance once he thought he knew all there was to know about the psyche.

Yet such a simplistic and therefore limited scientific approach cannot be maintained in the long run, despite the fact that it is still widely regarded as modern. Jung saw its end coming.

> The moment when physics touches on the "untrodden, untreadable regions," and when psychology has at the same time to admit that there are other forms of psychic life besides the acquisitions of personal consciousness–in other words, when psychology too touches on an impenetrable darkness–then the intermediate realm of subtle bodies comes to life again, and the physical and the psychic are once more blended in an indissoluble unity. We have come very close to this turning-point today.[72]

It has been indicated in the foregoing that this moment has in fact arrived for psychology as well as for physics. In psychology the collective unconscious and the archetype per se constitute a virtually "impenetrable darkness." Jung took cognizance of this by putting forward the hypothesis of the psychoid nature of the archetype and of the neutral realm in the background. In both these concepts "the physical and the psychic are once more blended in an indissoluble unity."

C. A. Meier has taken up the idea of the subtle body in order to shed light on the obscurities in medicine; even today psychosomatic relationships cannot be satisfactorily explained.

72. *Psychology and Alchemy*, par. 394.

The influence of the psyche on the body and vice versa is just as improbable as it is probable, and since a causal explanation does not lead anywhere, Meier has put forward the fruitful suggestion that psychosomatic relationships be regarded as synchronistic phenomena.[73] The organizing factor would then be the archetype of wholeness, which is as much physical as psychic and may thus be thought of as a "subtle body." Synchronicity, Meier says, "presupposes a *tertium*, higher than soma or psyche, and responsible for symptom formation in both–approximating to the theory of the 'subtle body.' "[74] It is the healer's task to take measures which are "favourable to the appearance of this 'third' of higher order, the symbol or archetype of totality."[75]

Meier also drew attention to a so far inexplicable experimental result for which the existence of a subtle body may yet offer an explanation. The Czech physiologist S. Figar made simultaneous plethysmographic investigations on the forearms of two persons in separate rooms who did not know of each other's presence. One of them was subjected to certain psychic stimuli which produced responses that could be registered in characteristic volume oscillations. The surprising thing was that in the case of the second person, who took no active part in the experiment, the plethysmograph registered volume oscillations which showed a significant congruence with those of the first.[76] Figar's experiments have been repeated in the United States on a larger number of subjects and with improved methods, and his findings have been fully confirmed.

The causalistic explanation would be that the ideas and "imaginations" produced by the psychic stimuli on the first

73. Meier, *op. cit.*, pp. 113–14.
74. *Ibid.*, p. 116.
75. *Ibid.*, p. 117.
76. *Ibid.*, pp. 112–13. *Cf.* S. Figar, "The Application of Plethysmography to the Objective Study of so-called Extrasensory Perception," *Journal of the Society for Psychical Research*, Vol. 40, 1959, pp. 162–72.

person formed a subtle body which caused measurable physiological changes in the second. But taking synchronicity as a principle of explanation, the inference would be that an archetype, which as a psychoid factor is itself a subtle body, manifested or "arranged" itself in the parallel events.

The phenomenon is in accord with the alchemical conception of *imaginatio* as a half corporeal, half spiritual being, whereby the soul is enabled to bring about "many things of the utmost profundity outside the body" by imagining them.[77] Michael Sendivogius says: "Moreover the soul by which man differs from other animals operates inside his body, but it has greater efficacy outside the body, for outside the body it rules with absolute power."[78]

The speculations of the alchemists led to a profound understanding of the world which science is only now beginning to eye with due respect. It is astounding that they were able, despite a total lack of modern scientific assumptions, to anticipate and build into their philosophy interrelationships which were verified only centuries later. So great a treasure house of knowledge does not come to one overnight—even though it may be hidden in the psychic background. Thus Jung's interpretation and understanding of alchemy throws a light also on the character and humanity of the old masters. The results of their laborings and imaginings give one some idea of the seriousness, devotion, and patience they dedicated to the opus.

Alchemy could hardly have provided so broad a basis for Jung's investigations of the unconscious, nor could it have played such a decisive role as a historical touchstone for his

77. *Psychology and Alchemy*, par. 396, quoting Sendivogius, "De sulphure," in *Musaeum Hermeticum* (Frankfort, 1678), pp. 601ff.

78. "De sulphure," p. 617: "Anima autem, qua homo a caeteris animalibus differt, illa operatur in corpore, sed majorem operationem habet extra corpus; quoniam absolute extra corpus dominatur."

insights, had there not existed a true affinity between him and the adepts of the hermetic art. "The experiences of the alchemists were, in a sense, my experiences, and their world was my world."[79] His experiment with the unconscious during the crucial years 1912–1919 was a true alchemical *imaginatio*. "The process through which I had passed at that time corresponded to the process of alchemical transformation."[80] His analysis and interpretation of countless alchemical texts, supported by a truly vast range of amplificatory material, culminated in a magnificent synthesis, a unitary vision of the whole. Thus the alchemist's injunction "solve et coagula," which might be paraphrased "out of dissolution, unity!" was followed faithfully to the end.

Even as a child Jung had "his stone," on which he would sit for hours, fascinated by the puzzle of which was "I"—he, the little boy, or the stone. For years it was "strangely reassuring and calming" to sit on his stone, "which was eternally the same for thousands of years while I am only a passing phenomenon."[81] For Jung the stone "contained and at the same time *was* the bottomless mystery of being, the embodiment of spirit," and his kinship with it was "the divine nature in both, in the dead and the living matter."[82] A cube-shaped stone, incised with inscriptions in his own hand, stands like an oracle before his Tower, Jung's country house in Bolligen[83] on the upper lake of Zurich, and the last great and solacing dream before his death was of the *lapis*. He saw "a huge round block of stone sitting on a high plateau, and at the foot of the stone were engraved the words: 'And this shall be a sign unto you of Wholeness and Oneness.' "[84]

79. *Memories, Dreams, Reflections*, p. 205.
80. *Ibid*., p. 209.
81. *Ibid*., pp. 20, 42.
82. *Ibid*., p. 68.
83. *Ibid*., pp. 226ff. and Plates VI and VII.
84. M. Serrano, *C. G. Jung and Hermann Hesse* (London, 1966), p. 104.

Yet, unlike the alchemists, what fascinated Jung his life long was not Matter, but Psyche. For the scientist in him she was the object of rigorous empirical research; as a physician he succored her with deepest understanding; as a man he was the master and servant of her transformations.

III.

C. G. Jung and National Socialism

Carl Gustav Jung is constantly being accused of having been an anti-Semite, a Nazi or friend of naziism, and even today the recriminatory voices have not fallen silent. The main points of the repeated accusations are his attitude toward the Jews, his acceptance of the presidency of the (allegedly German) Society for Psychotherapy, and his editorship of its organ, the *Zentralblatt für Psychotherapie*, after the Nazis came to power. These accusations appear all the more plausible as it is generally maintained that both the Society and the *Zentralblatt* were "conformed" (gleichgeschaltet) to the Nazi ideology, which entailed, above all, the rigorous exclusion of Jews from membership of the said Society.

The critical events took place more than thirty years ago, and in the meantime they have in part been forgotten and in part are known in full detail only to a few. In order to arrive at an objective judgment, so far as this is possible, it is necessary that the most important facts should be briefly surveyed again—facts which present favorable, as well as unfavorable, evidence about Jung.

When the Nazis seized power (1933) Professor Ernst Kretschmer, president of the General Medical Society for Psychotherapy (Allgemeine Aerztliche Gesellschaft für Psychotherapie), resigned. As with all scientific societies that were located in Germany, the *Gleichschaltung* of the "General Society" seemed only a matter of time. At this critical moment (June 1933), and at the urgent request of its leading members, Jung, then honorary vice-president, accepted the presidency[1] in the hope of being able to avert the worst. In acceding to his colleagues' request, Jung was in an altogether different situation from Kretschmer: as a Swiss he could accept the presidency without being bound by the Nazi ideology. Unlike Kretschmer, neither his intellectual nor his political freedom was at stake. But what only a few people know is that within a matter of months he had used his freedom as a Swiss to redraft the statutes of the Society so as to make it formally and effectively *international* in character.[2] In spite of this, it is still alleged today that Jung was president of a *nazified German* Society, and it is even maintained that he ousted Professor Kretschmer in order to spread the Nazi doctrine.

Before its reorganization under Jung the Society had already been international in membership, though it was dominated by the Germans, who held the main executive positions. Jung's amendment of the statutes, however, gave *de facto* existence to the "International General Medical Society for Psychotherapy," which was composed of different national groups or sections. Jung was president not only of this Society but also of the Swiss section. A separate German Society ("Deutsche allgemeine ärztliche Gesellschaft für Psychotherapie") had been founded in Berlin (September 1933), as the "conformed" German section of the International Society.[3] From then on the nazified German section was only one among numerous

1. *Zentralblatt*, Vol. VI, No. 3, December 1933, p. 142.
2. The statutes were subsequently ratified at a congress of the International Society at Bad Nauheim, May 1934. *Cf. Zentralblatt*, Vol. VII, No. 3, p. 124. By that time also the non-German members of the Society had constituted their national groups ("Landesgruppen").
3. *Cf. Zentralblatt*, Vol. VI, No. 3, pp. 140ff.

other national groups, having as its president the psychiatrist Professor M. H. Göring, cousin of the notorious Reichsmarschall. It is obvious that this relationship and the ominous name were sufficient in themselves to give rise to innumerable misunderstandings and misrepresentations considering the supercharged atmosphere prevailing at the time.

The *Zentralblatt für Psychotherapie*, which had been published in Germany since the inception of the original Society, was thereupon taken over as the organ of the International Society, whose headquarters were in Zurich, with Jung as editor. The following event put Jung into a very awkward situation: it had earlier been planned that Professor Göring would bring out a "Sonderheft der deutschen Gesellschaft," as a special German supplement to the *Zentralblatt*, for exclusive circulation in Germany. It was to contain a signed declaration by Professor Göring obliging the members of the German Society to adopt Hitler's political and ideological principles. Whether through negligence or by mistake (or, one asks retrospectively, by design), Göring's manifesto appeared not only in the supplement *Deutsche Seelenheilkunde* (Leipzig 1934) but, in slightly different form, also in the current December 1933 issue of the *Zentralblatt*—without Jung's having been apprised of this fact.[4] An issue appearing under his name as editor and carrying the Nazi manifesto was a grave embarrassment to him. In the eyes of the world it was even worse: the Swiss psychiatrist, Dr. Gustav Bally, launched a sharp attack on Jung in the *Neue Zürcher Zeitung* (27 February 1934) and therewith the discussion began.

One may have honest doubts as to whether Jung acted correctly in sitting down at a table with German doctors at that time of terror, even if he did so under the auspices of an international society. On the other hand, there was no other

4. *Cf.* Jung, "A Rejoinder to Dr. Bally," *Civilization in Transition* (Collected Works, 10; hereafter CW), p. 538.

conceivable way in which his German-Jewish colleagues might have been helped. We shall see that in due course Jung took vigorous steps in this direction. If we wish to form, so far as we can, an objective judgment, we must raise a question of principle which even today, thirty years after the event, has not received a definitive answer: Should the outlawing of an incriminated nation, and its spiritual isolation, be considered a necessary consequence of its crimes, or should one strive with as much right for spiritual and cultural collaboration in the interests of "coexistence"? Jung opted for collaboration with the doctors and psychotherapists of Nazi Germany and thus exposed himself to the judgment of his contemporaries and of posterity.

In his "Rejoinder to Dr. Bally," which, like Bally's attack, still makes instructive reading today, Jung set forth the personal reasons that led him to his decision: before everything else he was concerned to keep the young science of psychotherapy alive, which "at a single stroke of the pen in high places"[5] could have been swept under the table in Germany. For its sake he was willing to risk his person and his name. He was out to help suffering humanity, regardless of nationality and differences of political sentiment. The core of his defense is contained in the following words, which sum up his attitude at that time: "The doctor who, in wartime, gives his help to the wounded of the other side will surely not be held a traitor to his country."[6]

To judge of the difficulties faced by a scientific society during the years of the Nazi revolution one may take for comparison the fate of the Freud group of the Psychoanalytic Society in Nazi Germany. Paul Eitingon, the Jewish-Polish member of its executive committee, was replaced by the German "Aryan" Felix Boehm, and Freud declared himself in

5. *Ibid.*, p. 536.
6. *Ibid.*, p. 539.

agreement with Eitingon's resignation. In the same fateful year (1933), the Jewish members "voluntarily" seceded in order to "preserve the integrity of psychoanalysis in Nazi Germany." Lewis Mumford seized on these facts—they are reported in Ernest Jones' biography of Freud[7]—and compared them with Jung's all-too-tolerant attitude and his cooperation with the "Nazi-controlled German psychological society," calling it "a hardly less reprehensible Freudian parallel."[8]

But expressly in this connection it should be noted that one of Jung's first official acts as president of the International Society was the implementation of a statutory provision which worked in favor of his Jewish colleagues in Germany. At the Congress of the International Society at Bad Nauheim in May 1934, Jung stipulated that the German-Jewish doctors who had been ejected or excluded from the German section could individually become members of the International Society with equal rights, thus preserving their professional and social status.[9] Even though this measure later proved ineffective in the face of the Nazi terror, it was nevertheless Jung's intention

7. *Sigmund Freud*, Vol. III, pp. 182ff.

8. "The Revolt of the Demons," *The New Yorker* (May 23, 1964), p. 175.

9. The provision was communicated in the form of a "Circular Letter" inserted as a separate sheet in the December 1934 issue of the *Zentralblatt* (Vol. VII, No. 6): "Esteemed Colleagues: At the last Congress [Bad Nauheim, 1934] of the International General Medical Society for Psychotherapy, it was decided to constitute the Society in the form of national groups. Therefore, national groups have been formed or are being formed in the various countries that were represented at the Congress (Denmark, Germany, Netherlands, Sweden, Switzerland). The conditions of membership in these national groups vary according to the local bylaws. Because of the political circumstances and because national groups do not yet exist in all countries, so that individuals as such cannot join their respective groups, it has been decided that association with a national group is on a purely voluntary basis; in other words, individual membership is possible within the framework of the International General Medical Society for Psychotherapy. The International Society is neutral as to politics and creed . . . We therefore respectfully invite you to join the International General Medical Society for Psychotherapy. [signed] Dr. C. G. Jung." Quoted from *Civilization in Transition*, pp. 545–46.

to come directly to the aid of his Jewish colleagues in Germany in the teeth of the anti-Semitic restrictions promulgated by the Nazi regime. His stipulation that the Society be "neutral as to politics and creed" (*see* n. 9) affirmed its complete independence of the German section.

After the Bad Nauheim Congress and at Jung's special request his assistant, Dr. C. A. Meier of Zurich, secretary-general of the International Society (now Professor of Psychology at the Swiss Federal School of Technology, Zurich), was appointed managing editor of the *Zentralblatt*. Later, in 1936, when Professor Göring became co-editor of the *Zentralblatt*—a fact which is often mentioned as weighing heavily against Jung—it was due to Jung and Meier that the *Zentralblatt* was not "conformed," and it continued to publish unbiased reviews of books by Jewish authors, as well as contributions by foreign writers such as H. G. Baynes, Esther Harding, and C. Baudouin.[10] In 1938 the last congress of the International Society took place under Jung's presidency at Oxford. On this occasion the University of Oxford conferred upon him the degree of *Doctor honoris causa*. Jung's Presidential Address dealt with the points common to the different schools of psychotherapy; his aim was to give psychotherapy, on this common basis, "a well-merited place among the other branches of medical science."[11]

By 1939 the relationship of the German section to the other national groups had become very difficult indeed. When the Germans tried to overwhelm the Society with a large Italian, a Hungarian, and even a Japanese group, Jung demanded binding assurances regarding the non-application of the "Aryan regulations." As these were not forthcoming, he resigned from the presidency. Statutorily, the presidency should then have

10. *Zentralblatt*, Vol. VIII, No. 2, p. 165. *Cf. Civilization in Transition*, pp. 552–53.
11. *Ibid.*, p. 567.

passed to the vice-president, Dr. Hugh Crichton-Miller, of London; but in 1940 Professor Göring declared peremptorily and illegally that the International Society, together with the *Zentralblatt*, was "conformed" and transferred its headquarters from Zurich to Berlin.[12]

Jung's efforts on behalf of his German-Jewish colleagues, made in his capacity of president of the "International Society," were known only to a few people; but during those critical years he also helped countless individual Jews with advice and active support. These Jews, many of whom were or became his friends, have made this publicly known, and there is no need to go into details here. In 1934 he had included in his book *Wirklichkeit der Seele* (Zurich, 1934) a contribution by the Jewish author Hugo Rosenthal: "Der Typengegensatz in der jüdischen Religionsgeschichte" (The Type-Difference in the Jewish History of Religion) and in the same year he wrote a foreword to the book of his Jewish pupil Gerhard Adler: *Entdeckung der Seele* [Discovery of the Soul] (Zurich, 1934).

By his helpful activity Jung proved that he was anything but an anti-Semite. His strenuous efforts did not, however, prevent him from publicly pointing out, as a psychologist, the difference between Jewish and non-Jewish psychology. Because of the racial fanaticism in Germany at the time, this was taken as an expression of Nazi sentiment and continues to be interpreted even today as a further proof of Jung's anti-Semitism. No Jew who is conscious of himself as a Jew will deny that such a difference exists. But the fact that Jung dragged it into the limelight at this particular moment, when being a Jew was enough to put one in danger of one's life, and that he placed the topic of differences of racial psychology on the

12. *Cf. Hugh Crichton-Miller, a Memoir* (Dorchester, England), pp. 1–2; also letter from H. Fierz in the *Weltwoche* (Zurich), October 31, 1958, p. 7.

scientific program of the International Society,[13] must be regarded as a grave human error. Even though the most atrocious consequences of the hatred of the Jews became public knowledge only later, the slightest hint of Jewish "differentness" served at that time as fuel for further fanaticism. In this respect the medical discretion enjoined on every physician would have been the order of the day. The fact that Jung did not observe it accounts for the reserve many Jews feel toward his personality.

Besides this, in his writings at that period, Jung expressed views on the Jewish character and on Judaism which were false and gave offense. Above all, his assertion that "the Jew, who is something of a nomad, has never yet created a cultural form of his own . . . since all his instincts and talents require a more or less civilized nation to act as a host for their development"[14] has aroused much ill-feeling. Statements like this sprang from lack of comprehension of Judaism and Jewish culture which is scarcely intelligible today, though it was widespread then. Thus even Freud, the Jew, could assert in 1908: "We Jews have an easier time [than Jung], having no mystical element."[15] Freud knew so little of Judaism that he was totally unaware of the rich mysticism of the cabala and the mystic wisdom of Hasidism. A general interest in Judaism, particularly among non-Jews, was initiated–strangely enough –during the Hitler era and became still stronger with the founding of the state of Israel. From then on the works of Martin Buber, Gershom Scholem, Franz Rosenzweig, and many others have become known to a wider public. They helped to deepen a general knowledge of Judaism and Jewish culture or to explain them for the first time.

13. *Civilization in Transition*, pp. 533–34. "Editorial," *Zentralblatt*, Vol. VI, No. 3.

14. "The State of Psychotherapy Today," *Civilization in Transition*, pp. 165–66.

15. *Sigmund Freud*, Vol. II, p. 55.

For all the justified accusations leveled at Jung and for all our sense of disappointment, we should not forget that when he spoke of the difference of Jewish psychology he did not, like the Nazis, imply any "depreciation" of it. This is quite apparent from an unprejudiced reading of his formulations, but is frequently overlooked. Certainly Jung did not make it easy for his readers to see into his mind. When he wrote that the subjective premise, or the "personal equation" of the Jew implied "no depreciation of Semitic psychology, any more than it is a depreciation of the Chinese to speak of the peculiar psychology of the Oriental,"[16] this could easily be misunderstood by anyone who did not know Jung. Jung took it for granted that his readers were aware of his veneration for the Chinese mind and Chinese culture. Thus his comparison had just the opposite effect to the one intended: it aroused resentment and correspondingly distorted reactions, and soon one was reading in the press that Jung had compared Jews to a Mongolian horde![17]

Jung, to put it briefly, saw the Jews as a "race with a three-thousand-year-old civilization," whereas he attributed to the "Aryans" a "youthfulness not yet fully weaned from barbarism."[18] The former possessed in Jung's eyes the inestimable advantage of greater consciousness and differentiation, while the latter were closer to nature and capable of creating new cultural forms. For Jung the epithet "barbarism" meant anything but a compliment. It should also be remembered that long before the advent of the Nazis, psychological race differences had been a theme for discussion among psychoanalytic researchers and therapists. The first references to this appear in

16. *Civilization in Transition*, p. 534. "Editorial," *Zentralblatt*, Vol. VI, No. 3.

17. Ernest Harms, "Carl Gustav Jung: Defender of Freud and the Jews," *The Psychiatric Quarterly* (April, 1946), p. 17.

18. "The State of Psychotherapy Today," *Civilization in Transition*, pp. 165–66.

Jung's writings as early as 1913,[19] but they were never an expression of anti-Semitism. On the contrary, his statements were concerned with the fact that the "personal equation" had to be taken into account in psychology more than in any other science.[20]

> In psychology the object of knowledge is at the same time the organ of knowledge, which is true of no other science. . . . If the organ of knowledge is its own object, we have every reason to examine that organ very closely indeed, since the subjective premise is at once the object of knowledge which is therefore limited from the start.[21]

In other words, since it is the psyche that cognizes the psyche, a subjective element must attach to all psychological cognition, for which reason it is not a matter of indifference *who* it is that utters the "psychological truth." In his old age Jung was still emphasizing the subjective character of his own psychology as well as that of Freud, Adler, and others, as conditioned by individual type, time, culture, etc.[22] In his earlier years he even understood every psychology as a "subjective confession."[23] And with regard to psychoanalysis, which was of special concern to him because of his onetime collaboration with Freud, he never overlooked, any more than did its founder, the specifically Jewish component of its fundamental conceptions.

In a letter to Karl Abraham written in 1908, Freud stressed the Jewish character of his thoughts and of psychoanalysis as though it were self-evident.

19. *Ibid.*, p. 543 and n. 4.
20. *Ibid.*, p. 533.
21. *Ibid.*, p. 540.
22. *Memories, Dreams, Reflections*, recorded and edited by Aniela Jaffé, translated by Richard and Clara Winston (New York and London, 1963), p. 207.
23. "Rejoinder to Dr. Bally," *Civilization in Transition*, p. 540. *Cf.* also "Freud and Jung: Contrasts," *Freud and Psychoanalysis* (CW, 4), p. 336.

> Be tolerant and don't forget that really it is easier for you to follow my thoughts than for Jung, since to begin with you are completely independent, and then racial relationship brings you closer to my intellectual constitution, whereas he, being a Christian and the son of a pastor, can only find his way to me against great inner resistances. His adherence is therefore all the more valuable. I was almost going to say it was only his emergence on the scene that has removed from psycho-analysis the danger of becoming a Jewish national affair.[24]

At the word "Christian," Jones adds in a footnote: "The customary Jewish expression for 'non-Jews.' " Freud's words reveal the sentiments of a great Jew who had a deep knowledge of psychic relationships and looked beyond the human limitations of the moment. For *him* to acknowledge the Jewish character of psychoanalysis did not imply any depreciation of it! The succeeding generation mostly thought and felt very differently about this matter, and it is only recently that important Jewish thinkers have begun to understand that Freud's work is largely conditioned by his Jewishness. A short but highly significant analysis of its unconscious Judaistic basis may be found in an essay by Erich Neumann, "Freud und das Vaterbild."[25]

The fundamental importance of the "personal equation" has shown that in practice nobody is able to follow the way of individuation and achieve self-realization if he is not profoundly conscious of his historical as well as of his religious background, because individuality is rooted in the collective. Tradition, religion, and the sense of belonging to a community are among the basic requisites for any individuality, no matter whether the individual keeps faith with them or goes his own

24. *Sigmund Freud*, Vol. II, p. 53.
25. *Merkur* (Stuttgart; August, 1956). *Cf.* also Neumann's "In Honour of the Centenary of Freud's Birth," *Journal of Analytical Psychology*, Vol. I, No. 2 (London, May 1956).

way. But consciousness of their tradition and their roots no longer remained self-evident once the emancipation of the Jews had taken place. Thus, as we know, it was lacking also among German Jews in the pre-Hitler period. Many of them no longer felt themselves to be Jews but only Germans, and had forgotten their national and religious peculiarities. This led to the concept of the "assimilated Jew," which, for Jews conscious of their Jewishness, is a decidedly negative judgment. By contrast Jung asks: "Are we really to believe that a tribe which has wandered through history for several thousand years as 'God's chosen people' was not put up to such an idea by some quite special psychological peculiarity?"[26]

The final, and perhaps decisive, question in evaluating Jung's position is: What was his attitude towards National Socialism as a political movement? Some of his observations from the years 1933–34 lead one to conclude that he set his hopes on a fruitful development in Germany, and that he was willing to give National Socialism a chance in its early days. That the "Aryan" unconscious contains creative tensions and "seeds of a future yet to be born"[27] was the psychological foundation of his hopes. Only his deceptive hope that something positive might emerge from the chaos can explain Jung's attitude. Later he admitted this himself. In his "Epilogue to Essays on Contemporary Events" (1946) he wrote:

> When Hitler seized power it became quite evident to me that a mass psychosis was boiling up in Germany. But I could not help telling myself that this was after all Germany, a civilized European nation with a sense of morality and discipline. Hence the ultimate outcome of this unmistakable mass movement still seemed to me uncertain, just as the figure

26. "Rejoinder to Dr. Bally," *Civlization in Transition*, p. 541.
27. "The State of Psychotherapy Today," *ibid.*, p. 165.

of the Führer at first struck me as being merely ambivalent. . . . Like many of my contemporaries, I had my doubts.[28]

Some people, disappointed by Jung's attitude, expected a more circumstantial, perhaps more emphatic, "admission of guilt"; others took the very sobriety of this statement as proof of its sincerity. And it would indeed be a grave falsification of the facts to speak of Jung's guilt in identifying with the Nazi ideology. At no time was there any such identification even though in the beginning he was fascinated by the "formidable phenomenon of National Socialism."[29] Psychologically this mass psychosis represented an outburst of the collective unconscious, and as with his patients, Jung counted on the healing and creative forces inherent in the human psyche to do their work. He felt justified in this attitude because, as he says, the contents of the collective unconscious are themselves ambivalent.

> The driving forces of a psychological mass movement are essentially archetypal. Every archetype contains the lowest and the highest, evil and good, and is therefore capable of producing diametrically opposite results. Hence it is impossible to make out at the start whether it will prove to be positive or negative.[30]

In spite of his psychological knowledge Jung remained optimistic, which proves once again the truism that a great scientist is not necessarily a good politician!

In an interview[31] Jung compared the Führer to a medicine-man and drew attention to his magico-mystical qualities. This caused a great uproar and is still misconstrued today as praise.

28. *Ibid.*, p. 236.
29. *Ibid.*, p. 166.
30. "Epilogue to Essays on Contemporary Events," *ibid.*, p. 237.
31. "Diagnosing the Dictators," *Hearst's International Cosmopolitan* (January 1939). See p. 125, n. 12 below.

Yet when the German Resistance poet Carl Zuckmayer said exactly the same thing in his memoirs, that "Hitler was able to put people in a trance just like the medicine-man of a savage tribe,"[32] nobody took offense and nobody misunderstood him. Today it can no longer be doubted that naziism and its Führer were driven by the destructive, demonic forces of a fanatical pseudo-religious movement.

Later Jung admitted that in spite of his knowledge of the psyche he did have illusions about man: he could never have imagined an outbreak of such fathomless evil.[33] Yet he himself, long before the advent of Hitler, had warned in 1918 about "the blond beast menacingly prowling about in its underground prison, ready at any moment to burst out with devastating consequences."[34] But who took the warning seriously then? And in the decisive moment Jung himself had forgotten it.

After the fearful abysses of the Nazi regime had become known, Jung revised his hopeful and expectant attitude and was pitiless in his public criticism. In these later pronouncements on Germany there may also be heard the disappointment of a man who realized just how much he had jeopardized his reputation when he staked his personality, his work, his energy, and his hopes on collaboration with doctors and psychotherapists in Nazi Germany. It is true that this comes out most clearly in his essay "After the Catastrophe,"[35] which he wrote when the gruesome drama was over. But already in 1936, in his essay on "Wotan,"[36] he had branded naziism as a manifestation of the typical "furor Teutonicus," which he saw personified in Wotan the storm-god. In "Psychology and Re-

32. Carl Zuckmayer, *Als wär's ein Stück von mir. Lebenserinnerungen* (Frankfurt-am-Main: S. Fischer-Verlag, 1966).

33. Letter (April 1946). See p. 95, n. 42 below.

34. "The Role of the Unconscious," *Civilization in Transition*, p. 13.

35. *Ibid.*, pp. 194ff.

36. *Ibid.*, pp. 179ff.

ligion" (1937) he criticized very sharply the tendency to mass movements then discernible in Germany,[37] having previously warned about the dangers of this phenomenon in a lecture delivered in Cologne and Essen in February of 1933.[38] No wonder, then, that finally in 1940 his writings were suppressed in Germany and his name placed on the black list.[39] At that moment a stumbling-block to the Nazis was the fact of his having written a foreword to a book by his Jewish pupil Jolande Jacobi, *Die Psychologie von C. G. Jung* (Zurich, 1939).

I hope I have made it clear that despite his mistakes Jung was neither a Nazi nor an anti-Semite. This charge has already been rebutted on several occasions in the press, with supporting documentation. Nevertheless the legend of Jung's Nazi sympathies persists, and even today, thirty years afterwards, it is still held against him with undiminished virulence. Hence, besides setting forth the facts of the case we must raise the no less important question of the psychological reasons for the persistence of these attacks. An inquiry into the unconscious psychic background is thus unavoidable.

Criticism of Jung's attitude during the years 1933–34 is justified by the facts, as is evident from the account I have given. But it lends itself to counter-criticism when it gets overheated, is exaggerated and one-sided, and when it glosses over or denies everything positive and falsifies the facts. This kind of criticism is just as untenable as the opposite approach which turns a blind eye to Jung's mistakes during those years or considers them mere trifles.

37. *Psychology and Religion: West and East* (CW, 11), pp. 14–15, 28, 47–48.

38. "The Meaning of Psychology for Modern Man," *Civilization in Transition*, p. 154. *Cf.* also pp. 229–30.

39. *Ibid.*, p. 232.

For all those who have followed the anti-Jung polemics over the course of the years, the causes of the exaggerations and extenuations have become somewhat clearer, at any rate in their psychological aspects. One of the deepest roots probably lies in the relationship between Freud and Jung, which still exerts a peculiar fascination on people living today, and by no means only on psychologists of the Freudian or Jungian persuasion. The relationship between the two researchers was problematical from the start, and it ended tragically in mutual resentment which has never quite died out. Ultimately it was fruitful for both men and enriched them. In their friendship and separation, so spotlighted by the world, it was not only two great personalities that confronted one another in scientific and man-to-man discussion, not only the old master and the young disciple, but, above all, the Jew and the gentile. All this lent particular weight to their encounter and it explains the fervent interest which the world took and still takes in their relationship. It also explains the emotionality in evaluating it, the violence of the arguments pro and con.

The plethora of reviews of the book *Memories, Dreams, Reflections* is exceedingly instructive in this respect. The great majority of them concentrated on the chapter "Sigmund Freud," which is certainly not the most important one and gives the reader insight into only a small, if significant, segment of the essential Jung and his development. Most of the critics dished out the usual and generally accepted paradigm of Freud, the great fatherly psychologist, the creator of psychoanalysis, and Jung, the disciple, who betrayed and abandoned the "father" in order to tread his own wayward paths of which the "father" did not always approve. It is the typical, or archetypal, father-son relationship that was acted out by the two giants. Since every son, if he amounts to anything, will one day leave his father and perhaps outgrow him, it was inevitable that this cruel and tragic, but also perfectly natural, side of the father-son relationship should be enacted by the two protagonists.

In the eyes of many people Jung nevertheless turned traitor when he declined the mantle of the "successor" and "crown prince" (Freud's own formula!) which the "father" wished upon him, and chose instead to follow his own creative genius. In extreme cases the critics went to the length of diagnosing Jung's "Judas role,"[40] as though by separating from Freud he had betrayed a messenger sent by God. It is obvious and psychologically understandable that in any survey of the Freud-Jung relationship the contrast between Jew and gentile should play an important, indeed decisive part, and it is equally certain that this contrast casts a shadow on the appraisal of Jung's attitude to the Jews and to naziism. As I have attempted to show, Jung himself provided the cue for this. Yet criticism, if it is to be taken seriously, must stick to the facts. Only an unconscious emotionality that casts a veil over men's eyes can explain why it is that Jung's mistakes are assiduously overlooked by the one side and boundlessly exaggerated by the other. It also enables us to understand why people who condemn Jung for his alleged naziism and reject his work on that account can accept without qualms the philosophy of Martin Heidegger, unperturbed by the fact that he espoused naziism as a genuine Fascist at the University of Freiburg during the early years of the regime. This is no reflection on Heidegger's philosophy, a point we are not discussing; our sole concern is with the question of a differential judgment and its causes. Heidegger did not play the role of an archetypal figure before the eyes of the world. He was not the "spiritual son" of a venerated "spiritual father," whereas Jung's "apostasy"

40. Nandor Fodor, "Jung, Freud, and a Newly Discovered Letter of 1909 on the Poltergeist Theme," *The Psychoanalytical Review* (Summer 1963), p. 127.

wounded the "father," the great Jew, Freud. Does anybody ask himself whether the "son" might not have been equally wounded by this separation? It might also be remembered, as Jones reports,[41] that Freud himself was struck by the analogy with his own separation from his old teacher Breuer, though nothing is ever heard of Freud's "Judas role" in this connection.

Three decades have passed since the Hitler terror. Jung died in 1961, and in retrospect even his mistakes at that period fall into place in his life and work without diminishing the stature of his personality. To adopt the language of analytical psychology, one could speak of a manifestation of his shadow which, as an archetype, clings to every man and is often all the blacker the brighter the light his personality sheds. Jung gave mankind too much for his shadow ever to dim his spiritual significance and his greatness as a man.

A new source will become available in the not too distant future for those who wish to inform themselves of the general background: a selection of Jung's letters is to be published in about one year's time;[42] they most vividly reflect his attitude during the Nazi period. The tenth volume of Jung's Collected Works, *Civilization in Transition* (1964), containing the documents relating to the years when he was president of the International General Medical Society for Psychotherapy as well as his controversial observations on Jewish and German psychology should also contribute towards a clarification of the facts. It is to be hoped that an unprejudiced reading of these publications will finally dispel the charges of naziism and anti-Semitism, regardless of whether one rejects on principle Jung's

41. *Sigmund Freud,* Vol. II, p. 169.

42. In two volumes, 1906–1961 (Princeton University Press; and Walter-Verlag, Switzerland). The editing was entrusted by Jung to his daughter, Frau Marianne Niehus-Jung, since deceased, and to two of his Jewish pupils, Dr. Gerhard Adler and myself.

scientific collaboration with the German doctors or accepts it as an attempt to render aid "to the wounded of the other side," and however much one must regret his expectant attitude at the beginning of the Nazi regime and has to deplore the publicity he gave to psychological race differences at that time.

In the course of the years Jung revised and deepened his knowledge of Judaism. This is evident from his later works with the wealth of Jewish source material amassed by him. The unlimited support he gave to Jews and non-Jews alike during the critical years of National Socialism, and his personality as a man, are the basis upon which his Jewish pupils have reconciled themselves to his mistakes. Large numbers of them are living today, not only in Europe and America, but also in Israel, and are spokesmen for Jungian psychology.

As we have said, Jung the researcher was fascinated by the creative contents of the *collective unconscious*, and this positive valuation lay behind his hopes for a fruitful development of National Socialism, that explosion of unconscious forces. But in the course of time the decisive role of *consciousness* as the discriminating and responsible agent which assigns meaning to events became increasingly clear to him. Although consciousness—and hence also man's individuality—can develop creatively only when deeply rooted in the unconscious psychic background, the humanity of man depends on his consciousness and its attitude towards the nature-bound forces of the unconscious which are both healing and destructive. Consciousness alone decides whether it will cooperate with them or resist them. From the typological standpoint one could describe the revision of Jung's scientific views and the shifting of his values as the transformation of the "romantic" into the "classic," and might speculate that the "classic" Jung would never have given National Socialism the ghost of a chance.

Those who had an opportunity to converse with Jung personally were in a better position than an outsider to see the shadow side of this great researcher and to accept it. As evidence of this, I will quote from a letter which Gershom Scholem wrote to me in 1963 and has kindly permitted me to publish. It reports a conversation he had about Jung with Leo Baeck.[43] With this report of a subjective experience I will end my attempt to give an account and interpretation of the facts.

Jerusalem
7 May 1963

Dear Mrs. Jaffé:

As you are so interested in the story of Baeck and Jung, I will write it down for your benefit and have no objection to being cited by you in this matter.

In the summer of 1947 Leo Baeck was in Jerusalem. I had then just received for the first time an invitation to the Eranos meeting in Ascona, evidently at Jung's suggestion, and I asked Baeck whether I should accept it, as I had heard and read many protests about Jung's behavior in the Nazi period. Baeck said: "You must go, absolutely!" and in the course of our conversation told me the following story. He too had been put off by Jung's reputation resulting from those well-known articles in the years 1933–34,[44] precisely because he knew Jung very well from the Darmstadt meetings of the School of Wisdom and would never have credited him with any Nazi and anti-Semitic sentiments. When, after his release from Theresienstadt, he returned to Switzerland for the first time (I think it was 1946), he therefore did not call on Jung in Zurich. But it came to Jung's ears that he was in the city and Jung sent a message begging him to visit him, which he, Baeck, declined because of those happenings. Whereupon Jung came to his hotel and they had an extremely lively talk

43. Leo Baeck (1873–1956), rabbi and professor of religion in Berlin. During the Hitler era he remained with his Jewish community in Berlin until his deportation to Theresienstadt in 1943. In 1945 he emigrated to England.

44. Probably referring to "Editorial" (1933), "The State of Psychotherapy Today," "Rejoinder to Dr. Bally," from all of which I have quoted.

lasting two hours, during which Baeck reproached him with all the things he had heard. Jung defended himself by an appeal to the special conditions in Germany but at the same time confessed to him: "Well, I slipped up"—probably referring to the Nazis and his expectation that something great might after all emerge. This remark, "I slipped up," which Baeck repeated to me several times, remains vividly in my memory. Baeck said that in this talk they cleared up everything that had come between them and that they parted from one another reconciled again. Because of this explanation of Baeck's I accepted the invitation to Eranos when it came a second time.

Yours sincerely,

G. Scholem

IV.

From Jung's Last Years

When I became his secretary in the autumn of 1955, Jung had just turned eighty. His scientific work was all but finished, the harvest had been brought in. He was satisfied that he had said everything it had been given him to say, he used to tell people who asked about his plans for work. Only those who knew him well could detect a slight tone of resignation behind his words. No bounds could ever be set willingly to his questing and inquiring spirit, but his body was tired, too tired to stand up to the demands of another round of creative work.

Jung's health and vitality had been weakened by an attack of amoebic dysentery in India in 1938, and a severe cardiac infarct in 1944 was the next blow life dealt him. "It was then that life busted me, as sometimes it busts everyone!" The frontier to physical old age had been crossed. But, on each occasion, illness and the proximity of death rekindled his creative powers and new ideas sprang to life. After the journey to India his preoccupation with alchemy took a central place in an extraordinarily fertile period of scientific work. Recovery from the cardiac infarct was followed by a phase of intense intellectual activity. "On the Nature of the Psyche,"[1] *Aion*,[2]

1. In Collected Works, 8; hereafter CW.
2. CW, 9, Part II.

"Answer to Job,"[3] "Synchronicity: An Acausal Connecting Principle"[4]—some of his most important writings—appeared in quick succession. This series culminated in the two volumes of *Mysterium Coniunctionis*,[5] which he described as his last book. They were published in 1955 and 1956; he had worked on them for more than ten years. The fatal illness of his wife Emma—she died in November 1955—marked the time when his life was nearing its end.

In 1955 his tall figure was slightly bent and even gave an impression of fragility. Yet most people overlooked this, because it paled beside the massive strength, the powerfulness, that radiated from him; no one who ever met him could escape its aura. It was not the powerfulness of an authoritarian; Jung was too good-natured for that, too kindly, too outgoing even in old age, and his humor too infectious. Nor was it the powerfulness one associates with erudition or with a highly differentiated and richly endowed intellect; his respect for any genuine knowledge and any ability of others was too great—nobody allowed himself to be instructed with greater zeal than he did. Jung's powerfulness had very little to do with authority in the usual sense. What was so palpably impressive about him sprang from the superiority of a man who had engaged in a life-and-death struggle with the creative daemon and mastered him, but on whom the struggle had left its mark. This kind of powerfulness is profoundly human, does not arouse fear, is not crushing, does not embarrass or make you feel small, but changes you; it compels veneration and awe.

When I took up my duties with Jung I had known him for about twenty years—my analysis with him began in 1937, a few months before he went to India. In 1947 I was made the secretary of the C. G. Jung Institute in Zurich, which had just

3. In CW, 11.
4. In CW, 8.
5. CW, 14.

been founded. Even then the major and minor tasks Jung used to delegate to me were accumulating–letters, research in libraries, reports on offprints and manuscripts that were sent to him for criticism and which were piled mountain-high in his library. In 1950 he incorporated my psychological study, "Bilder und Symbole aus E. T. A. Hoffmanns Märchen *Der Goldene Topf*," in his volume of essays *Gestaltungen des Unbewussten* (Zurich, 1950). Visits and analytical sessions, as well as the work for Jung, had one thing in common: they took place in a protected area sealed off against everyday life, forming islands of peace in the flux of time. All that was now to change.

The imminent confrontation with external reality was reason enough for two introverts to consider the situation thoroughly and to make the necessary preparations. My "initiation" into my new duties–a month or so before I started work–was brief and surprising. I was expected, Jung explained, never under any circumstances to allow myself to be irritated by his anger, nor by his occasional "grumbling," his roarings and cursings! I was further expected not to try to make myself indispensable. In Jung's eyes this well-known female aim was nothing but a secret demand for power; and the conscious or unconscious craving for power was for him the dark shadow, the root of countless evils, above all in human relationships.

The old man's honesty, his regard for my sensibilities in warning me of his easily aroused anger and of his tendency to give vent to his annoyance, were an expression of his relatedness, in which consideration and hard driving both played a part. This duality in his nature was perfectly genuine and evoked trust and allegiance. Till then I had known nothing of Jung's violent side; our relationship had been quiet and harmonious. This was now a thing of the past. The relationship had changed; it became more real and hence more complete.

Refraining from making myself indispensable presented no great difficulties: I had merely to keep the office in order so that it could be run at any time by somebody else, and everything looked for could be found. Once when I failed in this assignment, Jung reacted in a manner I was to find typical of him. We had set up a UFO Archive (UFO: Unidentified Flying Objects, or flying saucers), consisting of numerous books and technical writings about UFOs, as well as photographs, newspaper clippings from all over the world, letters, reports of dreams, and Jung's own notes. They rapidly filled several bookshelves and five or six large files, which, for lack of space, I had to accommodate in two different drawers. One afternoon Jung could not find the picture of a UFO he wanted to show to a visitor—an annoying but not particularly important incident. Since I was working that afternoon in my flat, it would have been quite easy for one of the house servants to telephone me, and in two sentences I could have put the matter right. But that way out would never have entered his head. Whenever in a similar impasse this convenient solution was suggested, he rejected it. This was not due to his dislike of the telephone and other modern gadgets, but to his basic attitude to everything that happened: he preferred to let things develop in their own way. "Don't interfere!" was one of his guiding axioms, which he observed so long as a waiting-and-watching attitude could be adopted without danger. Situations in which interference was obviously required were decided exceptions. This attitude of Jung's was the very reverse of indolence; it sprang from a curiosity about life and events that is characteristic of the researcher. They happened and he let them happen, not turning his back on them but following their development with keen attention, waiting expectantly to see what would result. Jung never ruled out the possibility that life knew better than the correcting mind, and his attention was directed not so much to the things themselves as to that unknowable agent which organizes the event beyond the will and knowledge of man. His aim was to understand the hidden intentions of the organizer, and, to penetrate its secrets, no happening was too trivial and no moment too short-lived.

Jung possessed a small antique mortar of shining bronze, which he used as an ashtray. Smoldering matches sometimes flared up again and started to consume everything in the vessel. Anyone who solicitously tried to blow out the little conflagration was mockingly chided or gravely rebuked. Don't interfere! Jung had seen through him, for the game with the burning matches was a test he had devised to try people out.

Respect for life also characterized Jung's analytical work. Worried or depressed patients hoped in vain for exhortation or comfort. Jung gave them something else: he wanted to get them to integrate the necessary suffering into their lives, to accept and bear it as part of their wholeness—for without darkness and sorrow there is no life. To soothe it away or exclude it would rob them of a vital experience, while the core of the depression would remain and soon enough provoke new suffering.

Jung's attitude and his demand for wholeness were not always easy to fathom, nor was it a simple thing to follow the way he pointed out, the way of individuation and destiny. No wonder that now and then the unconscious lent a helping hand with its images. The sordid dream of a woman patient puts the situation very aptly. She dreamed that she was commanded to descend into "a pit filled with hot stuff" and immerse herself in it. This she did, till only one shoulder was sticking out of the pit. Then Jung came along, pushed her right down into the hot stuff, exclaiming "Not out but through!" When he discussed this dream in a seminar[6] at the Federal Polytechnic, Zurich, he did so with visible enjoyment, knowing that he was

6. *Psychologische Interpretation von Kinderträumen*, Winter 1938/39. Privately multigraphed.

giving a clue to a number of patients, male and female, attending it.

Jung followed the downward movement of life if it was in keeping with the intrinsic truth of the moment. Yet he could experience joy whenever it came his way as few were able to, and wholeheartedly joined in the joy of others. Only when one got to know him better, over the years, did one discover that he—a true "Till Eulenspiegel!"—was never without the canker of secret care, for he knew the play of life's pendulum, the inevitable compensation of "high" by "low." Have you "suffered a success?" he would ask at a suitable moment, half mocking, half amused. He saw where it would end. Suffering accepted can gradually change into strength, composure, serenity; joy that remains heedless can change all too quickly and all too often into sorrow and restlessness. Suffering is a challenge, enforcing self-transformation; joy is not, and it does so much more rarely.

Any kind of "joyful Christianity" or sentimental prettification exasperated Jung to the limit. Never shall I forget his outburst of scorn and anger over a card announcing the birth of a child, garnished with the customary embellishments. The sorrows of life, the wretchedness of the times, were alive and present for him every moment as realities that had to be endured. This open-eyed alertness he expected also of others.

Sometimes I would come to the analytical hour filled with some difficulty, a dream or something else of importance, and burning to talk to Jung about it. But that was not to be. Jung himself was filled with something and would begin talking, and once he was well into his story he forgot the time. There was no stopping him. A good deal of strength was needed to interrupt him in sessions like these and trot out one's own affair, which, of course, he never took amiss. I never possessed the strength, and few others did either. But those who did not interrupt him found—regularly, I should say—that a surprise was in store for them. When once they were gripped by the torrent of thoughts, images and experiences, intuitions and dreams, amplifications and interpretations, once they swam along with it, without giving a thought to the advancing hand of the clock, they would suddenly discover that Jung's words were relating more and more clearly and finally with the greatest precision to the very thing they had wanted to tell him about. They got the answer without having posed the question. "He has a terrific intuition," an Englishman once said of him. Naturally these sessions were exceptional; normally Jung was the most patient and attentive of listeners. But the days on which he did the talking had, if possible, a still deeper effect.

Although it might be regarded as "interfering with nature," Jung, being a doctor, did not of course disapprove of treatment by medication. Only, he was very chary of using sleeping pills, particularly on himself. Even when he was long past eighty, he felt the rare occasions on which he had to resort to a soporific as a "moral defeat," and this pained him. Usually he enjoyed a wonderful, deep sleep, and plenty of it, the result not only of his good constitution but of his close and positive communion with the unconscious. Sleep was the source of his psychic strength. Whenever this closeness to the unconscious —which he took entirely for granted—was disturbed, he was irritated, almost ashamed, as though the Great Mother had been affronted by her son. He then tried patiently to restore the relationship, to find the way back to sleep and the door of dreams. He best succeeded in doing this by altering the regimen of the day. If he was working on a manuscript, it would be laid aside, and visitors in the afternoon were called off. In this way the bondage to time was loosened. Time no longer counted, and he was free to let go, to sink into himself, to muse on the images and thoughts that arose in him. Generally the outward peace soon brought about a restoration of sleep. His disturbed sleep was most quickly restored in his Tower in Bollingen,[7] where in earlier years he would often spend weeks by himself. Above all it had been sailing, letting himself go with the wind, that brought relaxation and inner peace.

Once a simple young girl was shown into his consulting room, a schoolteacher from a village in Canton Solothurn. A doctor, personally unknown to Jung, had sent her to him. She suffered from almost total insomnia and was one of those people who agonize over having done nothing properly and not having met satisfactorily the demands of daily life. What she needed was relaxing. Jung tried to explain this to her, and told her that he himself found relaxation by sailing on the lake, letting himself go with the wind. But he could see from her eyes that she didn't understand. This saddened him, because he wanted to help her, and there was only this single consultation to do it in.

> Then, as I talked of sailing and of the wind, I heard the voice of my mother singing a lullaby to my little sister as she used to do when I was eight or nine, a story of a little girl in a little boat, on the Rhine, with little fishes. And I began, almost without doing it on purpose, to hum what I was tell-her about the wind, the waves, the sailing, and relaxation, to the tune of the little lullaby. I hummed those sensations, and I could see that she was "enchanted."

This was what he told the Swiss journalist Georges Duplain, many years afterwards, in an interview.[8] (As it was given in French, the last words are even more meaningful: "J'ai chantonné ces sensations. Et j'ai vu qu'elle était 'enchantée.' ")

7. *Cf. Memories, Dreams, Reflections*, recorded and edited by Aniela Jaffé, translated by Richard and Clara Winston (New York and London, 1963), Ch. VIII.

8. "Aux Frontières de la connaissance," *Gazette de Lausanne*, Nos. 208–11, 4–8 September 1959. The story appears in No. 210, Sept. 7.

The consultation came to an end, and Jung had to send the girl away. Two years later, at a congress, he met the doctor who had sent her to him. The doctor pressed Jung to tell him what kind of therapy he had used, because, he said, the insomnia had completely disappeared after the girl's visit to Küsnacht and had never come back again. It was a mystery to him how Jung had cured her in a single consultation. The girl had told him some story about sailing and wind, but he couldn't get out of her what Jung had actually done. Naturally Jung was rather embarrassed. "How was I to explain to him that I had simply listened to something within myself? I had been quite at sea. How was I to tell him that I had sung her a lullaby with my mother's voice? Enchantment like that is the oldest form of medicine."

In spite of his advanced years, it was not always easy for Jung to give way to the need for rest and to admit the necessity for limited work, let alone inactivity. This was not due to fussiness—no one was less fussy than Jung; what held him back was his feeling of responsibility to time itself. Paying attention to time was more than a need, it was a stern demand that could not be circumvented. Hence his royal punctuality. Appointments and invitations were kept to the minute; he never kept anyone waiting.

Although his work as a scientist and doctor took up the greatest and most intensive part of Jung's time, it was only the first among a group of activities which he felt were equally meaningful. Working in the fields and in the garden, traveling, driving and sailing, sculpting, painting, fantasying, as well as cooking and playing games, talking and much else besides were essential to him, each at its proper time. When I first visited Jung after his severe illness, he was lying on a couch on the veranda opening to the garden. Beside him, within arm's reach, were ripe corncobs piled up in a heap. Carefully and skillfully he was shucking them into a large brown clay vessel. Only wasted time and emptiness were a burden to him, though they too are part of the whole.

Jung was a good Swiss citizen. Nothing but illness could prevent him from casting his vote, even in old age, and every Swiss knows the sense of responsibility and consciousness of duty this entails. If Jung did not feel sufficiently oriented about the issues, he would summon Hermann Müller, the gardener-chauffeur who had been with him for years, and ask him to get some newspapers with informative articles. Often this resulted in a man-to-man political discussion. Jung belonged to the "freethinking" or Democratic party. It may be remarked parenthetically that he supported women's right to vote, a right hitherto non-existent in Switzerland and a subject of fervent disputes. Foreign newspapers came into the house on days of political crisis; and magazines, especially the English *Listener* and the American *National Geographic Magazine* and the *Atlantic Monthly*, satisfied his need for information on political and other matters.

As a young man, Jung had started a collection of engravings, bought mostly from the "bouquinistes" in Paris, where he worked under Pierre Janet at the Salpêtrière. A sizeable collection of small Asiatic sculptures was added later, and finally his valuable collection of alchemical books. All these enrichments to his life and his house were objects of his love, care, and responsibility. His sense of responsibility extended also to the small and even trivial objects of daily use, the pipes, pencils, penholders, the tube of glue and the writing paper. It was one of my duties to collect the unwritten sides of the letters he received and to put them on his desk in small bundles held together with office clips. He used them for insertions and additions in his manuscripts, which he wrote on folio sheets. The insertions he wrote on slips which he cut to size from those bundles with a large pair of scissors and then glued into the wide margin. No writing pad could ever have replaced the old sheets from letters, for nothing might be wasted. This echoed experiences from his childhood and youth: in his father's parsonage strict economy was the order of the day. As a student he had to get his money, or at least part of it, from the sale of antiques belonging to a relative. Jung knew what poverty was.

But there was something else too: objects possessed for Jung a meaning in themselves, so they had to be treated with special care. "Things take their revenge!" he once hurled threateningly at my head when I had mislaid or botched something—I no longer remember what. Things are part of the life and presence of a person, and they contribute to his aura. This was all the truer of Jung because he was an intuitive thinker, and for the intuitive the world of things is an abiding source of fascination. It was amazing how things often acted in a most peculiar way in his presence. Sometimes they seemed bewitched and could not be found again. In that big house this was no cause for wonder, but it was for Jung. "The blue tobacco jar has been magicked away again!" he would lament, using an expression coined by a schizophrenic. We agreed to look for the things that had been "magicked" away only in the most urgent cases. Generally it was in vain anyhow and a sheer waste of time, and besides, it was an absolute certainty that one fine day, often shortly afterwards, they would be "magicked" back again, lying there as if nothing had happened. Nothing ever got lost.

For anyone like Jung, who devoted so much care and attention to them, objects began to animate themselves, living a life of their own. They would start talking, and communicate things that remain hidden from others. Objects are not always inert; sometimes they seem to join in the game of life, to reflect the mood and thoughts of people. That is why old legends, as well as poets, tell of broken rings, of mirrors that crack by themselves, of pictures that fall down, of stopped clocks and many other happenings that announce important meanings to naïve minds. Jung too experienced the wonderful and profound connections between the macrocosm and the microcosm, the outer and inner reality. Who would ever have registered a dead fish on the shore, a rose-chafer fluttering at the window, a dying fire, or the formation of a cloud as significant events? Who would have noticed them at all?

In a letter (May 1957) he wrote: "'You should make friends again with the nearest things,' said Nietzsche and didn't. He was wafted away on the great wind, drunk with his own words. Even things, thanks to the meaning immanent in them, answer us as we address them. They are socially minded and afford us delightful company in hours and days of loneliness."

In his observation of the inner and outer world Jung was altogether naïve, completely unself-conscious and free of prejudice. Observation belongs to the world of sensation, which must be considered his "inferior function," his intuition and thinking being highly differentiated. Because of its closeness to the unconscious, the inferior function has secret access to the wellspring of creativity–the old fairy tale motif of Tom Thumb who succeeds in slaying the dragon, discovering the hidden treasure and marrying the princess. But creativity comes alive only when consciousness allies itself with the inferior function, for which reason it is often the old king (the ruling consciousness) who sets the hero the task and gives the reward.

As an outstanding thinker and investigator, Jung created new and differentiated hierarchies of order for things naïvely seen. He hardly ever let his subjective experiences, hunches, and observations rest at that. Only when they had been thought through to the limits of the possible, and their associations and backgrounds thoroughly investigated, was his creative impulse able to fulfill itself. Thus his observation of objects and their strange behavior became the starting point for scientific insights. This led to the establishment of a new principle of explanation complementary to causality—the principle of synchronicity.

Jung's predilection for going along with the current of life, his careful observation of events great and small, of outer and inner realities, did not mean following a straight line or some infrangible law of action, nor did he favor it. On the contrary, Jung was highly inconsistent and well aware of this fact. Many formulations in his writings seem inconsistent too. But as the nature of the psyche is not straightforward and does not always obey the laws of logic, these inconsistencies are only apparently out of place; they reflect psychic truth better than straightforward thinking. So it was high praise, though of an unusual kind, when Jung informed me one day that I had been gloriously inconsistent. Jung's inconsistency was a stumbling-block to many, a reason for denigrating his work and shunning him as a man. It did indeed give me some hard nuts to crack, especially because it was his powerful personality that determined the course of action in daily life. The others followed. But anyone who followed long enough would discover immanent laws that held the apparent contradictions together. If I had done something to his satisfaction and wanted to do it the same way next time, it was in his eyes definitely not the right way. The right way was only what sprang up, new and spontaneous, at any moment. The right way was always the truth of the moment—even in daily work. If I succeeded in doing it thus freely, taking it as a kind of serious game, I found the experience much more enriching than when I did it as a matter of routine. It did not become more strenuous, as might be supposed, but was less tiring, because relaxation was demanded all the time.

Jung's way of life took the highway and the byway, harmony and disharmony, as self-evident and equally significant. He could speak with biting scorn of the "ideal of harmony" that hovers before many people—they are often "feeling-types"—because it is not in accord with the truth of life and the truth of man. In the long run it cannot be kept up; sooner or later it comes to a disappointing end, turns into disharmony. To Jung it seemed better, more honest, and wiser to look the possibility of disharmony in the eye and, once it had got that far, not to evade it, but rather to try to overcome it by frank discussion followed by an understanding silence. He liked to tell the story of the little daughter of one of his patients. Her parents lived in permanent and unclouded harmony. There was never a loud word spoken, they were cultured, comfortably off, and orderly in their lives. The little girl often used to visit some neighbors, staying there longer and longer and, finally, the whole day. Not for a long time was the reason discovered for her strange behavior, as the child still doted on her parents and brothers and sisters. Elvira (the neighbors' Italian maid), she explained to her mother, Elvira swore so marvelously and was always so excited! That was the enjoyment she had been seeking and missed at home. The perpetual harmony had a paralyzing effect or had simply become boring. Perhaps she had also sensed what lay hidden behind the harmony. Jung had a high opinion of the undistorted judgment of children and the sensibleness of their reactions.

What Jung meant by two people "having it out" with each other requires the greatest honesty. Neither should push the guilt on to the other, and neither should let the other deprive him of the "dignity of his guilt."

Only in collective relationships, in an impersonal group, did Jung expect reserve in the expression of subjective feelings and the control of emotion. In any collectivity emotions are dynamite; they easily lead to senseless squabbles and make collaboration difficult if not impossible. In a group, emotional adaptation—which can very well go hand in hand with independence and objective criticism—is the prerequisite for fruitful work.

Jung gave free rein to his emotions, both positive and negative, with his friends and in daily life. In his younger years his laughter rang out far and wide like a fanfare. Once there appeared on the terrace of Casa Eranos in Moscia, where the Eranos meetings were held every year in August, an amiable stranger, no longer young, whom none of the participants knew. He excused himself for intruding and explained why he had come: he wanted to meet the man who was laughing so heartily and uproariously that he, walking alone on the road to Brissago, high above Casa Eranos, had irresistibly been infected by it. Naturally Jung was enchanted and instantly engaged the stranger in conversation.

As a pendant to this little episode, there is Albert Oeri's recollection of Jung as a student: "Jung's binges were rare but loud."[9] Nobody enjoyed laughing as much as Jung; nobody made others laugh as he could. After the death of his wife his laughter became rarer and quieter.

But his humor and love of fun did not prevent things from slipping into another key, and then grumbling and railing were the musical accompaniment of the day. Jung never passed over the mischievousness of any object, never overlooked any mistake however trivial. And once you start looking for mistakes there is no end to them. At bottom the grumbling was a

9. Albert Oeri, "Ein paar Jugenderinnerungen" in *Die Kulturelle Bedeutung der Komplexen Psychologie*, Festschrift zum 60. Geburtstag von C. G. Jung. (Berlin, 1935), p. 524–28.

safety valve, a reprimanding of the thousand imps that botch a man's work and addle his thinking. In the early days of my secretaryship I was often on tenterhooks as Jung read through the letters I had put before him for signature. Every typing mistake was reproachfully and copiously commented on, but what a recompense it was when in his zeal he went too far and found himself in error! I soon learned to turn the tables on him and use the weapon that never failed: I made him laugh, or at least tried to. When a tempest had really broken loose, however, this weapon no longer worked, and then there was no recourse but to ask oneself, in all seriousness, how one had precipitated the storm, and stand up to it. In spite of his preliminary warning it was anything but easy to let his rage pass over my head. But if I succeeded and managed to appear for work the next day unshaken and unhurt, nobody was more grateful than he. Although most times no further mention was made of the tempest, now and then, often very much later and always when I had ceased to think about it, a word was dropped, or something unexpected happened, that expressed his thanks. The preciousness of these responses caused the importance of the bygone to shrink to nothing. But it was wise not to forget it. The rare occasions when "gale force ten" was reached, Jung out of genuine magnanimity begged my pardon.

His impatience was due not only to his temperament—astrologically he was a Leo—but also to his extreme sensitivity, which both enriched and burdened his life. It was an enrichment because it gave him the extraordinarily differentiated awareness I have already spoken of; it was a burden because it encroached upon the personal realm and manifested itself as touchiness. Jung was touchy, his feelings were easily hurt and needed sparing in order to display themselves. As usually happens, he found the weaknesses of others which were also his own the hardest to bear. Once he gave me a violent scolding for my sensitiveness and accused me of a secret lust for power. Sensitiveness was always demanding and tyrannical! Shortly afterwards I had a dream in which I was painfully aware of a tiny golden ball under seven mattresses—a veritable princess on the pea! When I told it to Jung, there was naturally a roar of laughter. But then he became serious and began telling me about himself and the sensitiveness that had tormented him from early youth, how it had encumbered him in his relationships and made him unsure of himself, how ashamed it had made him feel, but how, because of this same impressionability, he had perceived beauties and experienced things other people scarcely dreamed of. Doubtless his sensitiveness continued to plague him in later years, though then he no longer fought against it but gave it the most natural expression in joy, sorrow, and anger. This directness was a safety valve through which he set himself free for more important things. In the language of the East, it made him inwardly still and "empty."

To be fair to Jung, his impatience must be seen against the background of his patience. What patience it needed to wait literally decades until he had done everything in his power to substantiate his scientific discoveries before publishing a word about them![10] How much patience he had to summon up in order to set his analysands on the right path; how much patience with the world, the reading public, with the critics who constantly misunderstood him; and finally how much patience with himself, with his creative daemon, and not least with his own body, which gradually began to fail him.

"Only the wounded physician heals," says a piece of Aescu-

10. For instance, in the case of his mandala researches Jung wrote: "I have observed these processes and their products for close on thirty years on the basis of very extensive material drawn from my own experience. For fourteen years I neither wrote nor lectured about them so as not to prejudice my observations." From *Psychology and Alchemy* (CW, 12), par. 126. *Cf.* also "Synchronicity" (CW, 8), par. 816.

lapian wisdom. Jung's patience, wrested again and again from his impatience, was exemplary. The way of individuation he taught to pupils and analysands alike demands the highest degree of patience. How often one heard his alchemical exhortations: "Omnis festinatio a parte diaboli est" (all haste is of the devil), or "In patientia vestra habetis animam vestram" (in your patience you have your soul).

Jung was a decided visual type; the auditive faculty was recessive. However, it is not true, as is often asserted, that he was unmusical, though his feeling for music was influenced, and sometimes disturbed, by his sensitivity. Bach, Handel, Mozart, and the pre-Mozartians were pure joy to him. He had a penchant for Negro spirituals. There was one occasion when Schubert's string quartet in D Minor, which he was listening to on his new record player, had to be turned off because it moved him too much. Beethoven's sonatas distressed him, and the late quartets churned him up almost beyond endurance. The record player wasn't often used. But whenever a concert pianist gave a recital on the grand piano at the house in Küsnacht—the last one was the Russian, Ania Dorfmann—he was impressed by Jung's genuine feeling for music.

Personalia never played a prominent part in Jung's life; the real and important thing was the impersonal. Once when in a consultation I wanted to tell him about my relation to my parents—the *pièce de resistance* of a classic analysis—he wouldn't let me get a word out. "Don't waste your time! Anyway I know a person's relation to his parents at first glance!"

This is not to say that other analysands did not have to tell him in detail about their parental relationships—there was no rule. Although personal factors took a back seat in my analysis, they were taken into account when the need arose. This was the case in the thirties, when Jung would give me, an emigrant, various jobs to do as a means of earning money. He asked no fee for my analysis.

No externals were ever overlooked if they happened to be the patient's problem. No physical weakness, no fluctuation in health escaped his eye. Then the clinician in him awoke, and the trouble was investigated from the physical and psychic side with the same care and conscientiousness as were purely psychic problems. It goes without saying that he did not meddle with the competence of medical specialists. The same thoughtfulness was displayed in small things as well. If a guest came to him tired and on edge in Bollingen, he would, after a few words, lodge him in a deck chair by the lake, spread a blanket over him, and leave him alone for an hour until he had rested.

Generally speaking it is the personalia that arouse interest and curiosity. One hopes to penetrate into the life of the great and nose out the secret of their eminence through knowledge of outward particulars. In Jung's memoirs the personalia are almost entirely lacking, to the disappointment of many readers who missed the usual chit-chat about his relations with those closest to him. This criticism and the charge of Jung's "unrelatedness" were beside the point. His eye was always turned to the impersonal, the hidden archetypal background which he was willing to reveal only so far as it concerned his own life. If he claimed the right to keep quiet about his personal life and refused to make concessions to the wishes of the public, of which he was very well aware, he was only being himself. His silence safeguarded his private relationships.

Burning letters in the beautiful old stove with green tiles which stood in his library was a solemn and at the same time cheerful occasion. Once, with the fire roaring, he smote the side of the stove with the flat of his hand, as though clapping an old friend on the shoulder, and remarked, laughing: "This fellow is my discretion!"

Jung possessed a phenomenal memory. That he could still remember the dreams of his earliest childhood when he was well over eighty is astonishing enough. After he had recounted them for the memoirs, notes of the same dreams were found which he had written some forty years earlier, and they differed in not a single detail from the spoken versions. Sometimes even the wording was nearly the same. Jung could never get over my astonishment. Experiences of the inner world, he explained, above all of dreams, had engraved themselves indelibly in his memory as with a stylus. It was exceptional for him to tell the same dream in different versions. Likewise, his memory for objective facts, dates, names, places, ideas, things read and heard was unsurpassed and formed one of the foundations of his immense store of knowledge. But his memory failed when it came to personal matters. Then he often seemed like the proverbial absent-minded professor and remained clueless in the face of expostulations like "But you *did* say that" or "But it's all been arranged," and so on. "Thank God my memory does not burden me with personal things," he used to exclaim with relief. He also immediately forgot the well-known emotional and transference complications typical of any analysis, and this worked out fruitfully and salutarily both for him and the analysand. It was always the truth of the moment, whether positive or negative, that prevailed, and from the many moments of truth there gradually crystallized out the truth of the whole.

It was a great pleasure to be with Jung at the Eranos meetings. Pupils and patients turned out in full force, generally about a dozen of them, the female sex predominating, and it was nothing to us that because of this retinue we were decried as "Jungfrauen" or, occasionally, "maenads." Our good repute was the price we were quite willing to pay. We had little opportunity to talk with Jung outside the consulting hours, but here a little band was formed that remained together during the ten-day meeting, whose cohesive strength derived from the common experience of the lectures. Jung was wonderfully lavish with his thoughts; we could ask as many questions as we liked. The lecture hall opened on to a terrace separated from the garden and the lake by a low stone wall. In the half-hour interval during each lecture, and again when the lecture was over, Jung used to sit on this wall, and in a flash we were clustering round him like bees round a honey-pot, much to the annoyance of the other participants, whose circulation of the terrace was considerably impeded. But for us there began a game of question and answer which was the sheerest joy. Jung, too, took visible pleasure in our gatherings, though naturally he did most of the talking; however short and simple the question, it received an answer that spiralled round the theme and spread out in ever-widening circles. These "wall sessions" were the unforgettable highlights of the summer. They acquired a different character when Erich Neumann, of Tel-Aviv, was there, for then a dialogue developed between the two, and we listened.

In the first years of the meetings Jung used to stay on Monte Verità, Ascona, in Casa Semiramis. Later, when the walk and even the drive to Moscia began to tire him, Mrs. Olga Fröbe-Kapteyn, the founder of the meetings, placed at his and his wife's disposal the sunny little flat above the lecture hall that stood on the same piece of land by the Lago Maggiore where she herself lived in Casa Gabriella. From then on Jung would often invite us to visit him, either because the wall session had not been complete or because he wanted to tell us about the new thoughts that were running through his head. Generally they revolved round the lecture or one of the talks at the table in front of Casa Gabriella, where each day the lecturers sat together in the open air.

Once—it must be twenty years ago now—there was a

nocturnal celebration on the terrace of Casa Eranos, which lives on to this day as the legend of the "Nekyia." There was a great deal of merriment and noise, and although no music "invited to the dance," the merrymaking resounded far over the lake. Neighbors far and wide sent messages to Mrs. Fröbe, complaining about this unwonted disturbance of the peace, but in vain. Jung was slightly tipsy, and so were all the others—rather more so than less. He was thoroughly enjoying himself, encouraging those who were still too sober to pay due homage to Dionysus. He was here, there, and everywhere, bubbling over with wit, mockery, and drunken spirit. Only a poet could describe this gay and abandoned "night-sea-journey," the only revel that was ever held at Eranos. The epithet describing us as "maenads" was coined, incidentally, that night.

Jung had a passion for travel. All his life he wanted to know more about the earth, its countries, and its races. In his memoirs he reports on his travels to Africa, India, and the United States. He supported with all his powers every realizable plan of his pupils for travel. Once I planned a Mediterranean trip that would take me to Tunis and Algiers and finally to the longed-for goal, the Sahara. Jung was all afire and helped me to overcome my misgivings and anxieties. Two weeks before my departure I had an anxiety dream. I found myself in a mountainous region of Africa. Suddenly there was a dull rumbling, the earth quaked and hurled me down a steep slope. I shot into the abyss at terrific speed, but suffered no injury. Afterwards the earth settled down again. Naturally I was very frightened. Since I was conscious of my anxiety, the unconscious had no need to parade it again before my eyes. So what did the dream mean? My friends—psychologists and nonpsychologists—to whom I told it urgently advised me to cancel my plans, the unconscious had to be listened to, its warning taken seriously. Not so Jung: no question of letting the plan drop! Of course I must go on the trip, I had also to accept the risk of danger. The unconscious was nature, and like nature it could either help man or destroy him. What mattered was that he should try to confront nature consciously, to fathom it and transform it. That was the whole venture of life.

It turned out to be a marvelous journey. I did not think about the dream at all until the news of the earthquake in Agadir reached us. Though our safari was far away from Agadir, we were shaken by the report of the catastrophe.

Few people are really interested in accounts of their friends' travels. The endless photographs and postcards are a favorite theme for comic jokes after the holiday is over. Jung was an exception. He followed the story with tense interest, every photograph was thoroughly examined and often stirred memories and associations of his own. So the journey was lived through again in talking with him, and now and then details were rediscovered that had been overlooked.

Jung was a brilliant raconteur, and it was a joy to listen to him as he told of the experiences he had met with on his own travels. In his old age it pleased him to go on tours in Switzerland, accompanied by his American friend Fowler McCormick, who drove the car, and an old friend of the family, Miss Ruth Bailey, who after the death of his wife kept house for him. The prehistoric sites, and the remains of Roman and Romanesque culture, were favorite objectives, and the good cooking in the country inns where he rested was much appreciated. In his youth, when he traveled to Italy by bicycle, he used to stop off at inns where lorries were parked outside. He speculated that truckdrivers were no dainty eaters and knew which innkeepers served up something tasty.

Back from his tour, he would postpone our work and with

easygoing expansiveness recount all that he had seen and done. His undiminished pleasure, his lively interest and memory were eloquent of his sturdy life-affirmation.

Ordinarily Jung spoke in Basel German, which to my ears, accustomed to High German, sounded like a merry warbling. He was overjoyed whenever he met anyone who could speak the Basel dialect, together with the locutions that have fallen out of use, as well as he could. Occasionally he corresponded in undiluted Basel German, for instance with Prof. Rudolf Bernoulli. He spoke High German with me. He had a strong affinity for English, which he spoke fluently and loved. As his works had met with wide acceptance in the United States and England, his English correspondence was at least as copious as the German. He liked peppering Basel or High German with English words. His mellifluous and idiomatic French lacked merely the sense of affinity that bound him to English. Latin and Greek texts he read fluently, though he would enlist help when preparing translations for publication. Before going to Africa in 1926 he learned Swahili, which stood him in good stead during palavers with the natives in Kenya and Uganda. He had no Hebrew, which he regretted very much, especially after he became acquainted with the texts of Jewish mysticism, which he would have liked to have read in the original. But it seemed to him too late to start studying a new language. He had a smattering of Arabic, probably acquired in youth from his father, Pastor Paul Jung, who had graduated not as a theologian but as an Arabist.

With his children, grandchildren, and children-in-law he had warm ties. After the death of his wife, his four daughters and his daughter-in-law—each the center of a large family of her own—took turns staying with him for a while, to keep him company. In earlier years his son, who now lives with his family in the Küsnacht house, was his best sailing companion, and up to the end father and son formed a well-attuned team in the country life at Bollingen.

As I sat for the first time in the office of the Küsnacht house—it was on the ground floor between the kitchen and the fine large dining room, with a window opening on to the garden and the lake—I waited tensely for what was about to come. Jung had given me permission to read the copies of his letters, so the time passed quickly. At ten o'clock he appeared, and that was the hour when our daily work began. Generally it lasted until midday. I could hear his slow, rather dragging step as he passed through the hallway. I must confess that the approach of the old magician never lost its excitement in all those years. With my inner ear I still hear it to this day.

Two things I had to do that first morning. Because of his wife's severe illness the atmosphere in the house was muted, and it touched me to see how Jung took over the function of the master. A new cook had just been engaged, and Jung dictated to me the luncheon and dinner menu for every day of the week. Then we went upstairs to the library. Pulling a little key from his pocket, he opened a narrow safe let into the wall, which he called his "cache," and took out the four fragments of the bread knife that had exploded with a loud bang when he was experimenting with occultism as a student. He asked me to mount the four pieces as one, and with that I was dismissed.

Jung's correspondence was immense, and a frequent occasion for complaints and grumbling. It was obvious that dictating letters tired him, but they took an important place in his life. As his libido stopped flowing into the production of scientific works, they became a receptacle for his creative ideas, and so their number continually increased in his later years. Above all, they formed a link with the world, and that reconciled him, living as he did a withdrawn, introverted life, to all the labor they entailed. He also needed to get letters, he had to admit; and when, out of misplaced consideration, I forwarded too little post while he was on holiday, I earned an appropriate rebuke. Often the letters contained questions about his writings, or comments on them, and thus brought him an echo of his work, which he, like every creative person, needed. Although misunderstandings had to be reckoned with, and the reactions were not always favorable, they were nevertheless proof that his voice was being heard, and his work read and discussed.

It may be that he needed an echo from the world more than others did, because, for all his fame, so far as the scientific establishment was concerned he remained an outsider to the end, and this caused him considerable pain. But at bottom he understood and accepted his "outsiderness," because he knew that his ideas expected too much of his contemporaries. "I have never counted upon any strong response, any powerful resonance, to my writings," he says in his memoirs. "They represented a compensation for our times, and I have been compelled to say what no one wants to hear. . . . I knew that what I said would be unwelcome, for it is difficult for people of our times to accept the counterweight to the conscious world."[11] Any success amazed him, however much he enjoyed it and however annoyed he might be by dim-witted critics and reviewers. And yet, to be understood and accepted by the world was and remained a constant lure. Never, or only when physically debilitated, could Jung turn down a journalist who asked for an interview. Each time there was a lot of hemming and hawing, but in the end nearly everyone got his appointment. It was only to be expected that Jung was sometimes disappointed or irritated by the result, especially when the interview was published without having been submitted to

11. *Memories, Dreams, Reflections,* p. 222.

him first. He could never get it into his head that his language, his way of thinking, was not easy for outsiders to understand, and that the powerful impression made by his words, his voice and gestures, and the whole effect of his personality deceived the listener: he thought he understood what in reality remained dark to him. Jung was all the more pleased and grateful for the successful interviews, such as those with Mircea Eliade, Georges Duplain, Georg Gerster, Gordon Young, Richard Evans, and John Freeman.[12]

Jung seldom initiated a correspondence, but in later life his sense of responsibility bade him answer nearly all the letters that reached him from the outside world—private letters came under other rules. A distinguishing mark of his correspondence is that the great bulk of it was conducted with people unknown to him. Letters to the well-known or famous were in the minority. He never disdained to answer the questions of an unknown woman or a quite simple man, to explain to a young girl something she didn't understand, or even to give advice to a prisoner. For an American who described himself as "just a little fellow, fifty-eight years old and employed as a packer," he did his best to answer the question: What did he think about reincarnation. He was delighted whenever he discovered that his ideas had reached the people. It was one of Jung's exaggerations to say that the "man of the people" understood him better than the intellectuals, and he liked to tell the story of a poor and uneducated woman who wrote that she wanted to see him just once in her life. She ran a little newsstand with her brother in some small town. Jung invited her to come, and when he asked her if she had read his books, she replied: "Your books are not books, they are bread." Or the story of the little Jewish traveling salesman who stopped him in the street outside his house, looked at him with great dark eyes,

12. These and other interviews will be published by Princeton University Press.

and asked: "Are you really the man who writes those books? Are you truly the one who writes about these things no one knows?"[13] It was a particular joy to him that an abbess in Alsace read his "Answer to Job" with her nuns.

Naturally Jung, like all psychiatrists and psychotherapists, got a number of unanswerable letters from disturbed or psychotic people. But sometimes among them were letters that deserved special consideration, such as those from a seventy-year-old spinster bearing the name of an old Zurich family. Jung had seen her only once a few years earlier and diagnosed senile schizophrenia. She wrote to him every second or third day, sometimes daily, using small sheets of cheap, lined paper and cheap gray-green envelopes. Her clear, upright, childish writing was as if engraved. The content of the letters was always the same: she drew the *I Ching* hexagram she had thrown—she used this ancient Chinese book of oracles practically every day—and wrote a short commentary which connected the hexagram with herself, with Jung, and with world politics. Naturally there wasn't enough time to read all her letters. But he insisted on preserving them. Over the years they filled the drawer of a fine old mahogany cupboard almost to the brim. One day the letters stopped, and a little later I read of the death of the old lady in a newspaper. Afterwards I opened the last letter to find its way into the cupboard and saw, amazed, hexagram No. 11: "Peace." Her commentary consisted of a single sentence: how astonishing it was that in a time of trouble and pain the *I Ching* had answered with such a comforting sign. Jung was less impressed by the *I Ching*'s answer than I was; such happenings and interconnections seemed to him wonderful, but not more wonderful than nature. I understood then why he had given the letters asylum in his house: it was a symbolic gesture. We simply don't know

13. Both stories in Duplain, "Aux Frontières de la connaissance" (see p. 106, n. 8 above), No. 209, 5/6 September 1959.

the effects it may have when somebody's spirit is accepted even without any concrete reaction and merely through an act of empathy. It was remarkable enough that the lonely old lady had been able to preserve herself to her life's end without being hospitalized. Even after her death the letters remained untouched in the cupboard.

After 1956 only minor scientific writings were produced: an essay on flying saucers,[14] an article on schizophrenia,[15] "The Undiscovered Self,"[16] an article on conscience,[17] and finally a comprehensive account of the main ideas in his work, destined for publication in England.[18] Jung wrote it in English, because, he said, this forced him to express himself with the greatest simplicity. It was completed only a few weeks before his death. Our work together on the memoirs had begun in 1957, and I have given an account of its genesis in the introduction to that book. It cost him a mighty effort to reveal himself to the world as openly and unreservedly as his sense of responsibility required him to do, and when he called the memoirs a "purgatory" he was speaking in bitter earnest. Seeing his obvious distress, I suggested one day that we end our talks, and rest content with what had already taken shape, which by then had attained considerable proportions. But Jung wouldn't hear of stopping or giving up. It was inevitable, he replied, that people would write about him, and so he wanted to have a hand in it himself and do what he could for truth's sake. He was anxious to be understood, and he was well aware of the difficulties both he and his life presented to the world in the way of understanding. Contrary to his usual habit, he

14. "Flying Saucers: A Modern Myth of Things Seen in the Skies" (CW, 10).

15. "Schizophrenia" (CW, 3).

16. In CW, 10.

17. "A Psychological View of Conscience," *ibid.*

18. "Approaching the Unconscious," in *Man and his Symbols,* ed. by C. G. Jung (London and New York: Aldus Books, 1964).

never expressed an opinion, either positive or negative, about any of the chapters that were written during the following months.

When Jung was writing, he enclosed himself in an invisible shell. Nothing could distract him or break through his concentration; it was a cardinal law that he was never under any circumstances to be spoken to while writing. I often happened to be busied in the library when he sat down at his desk. It did not disturb him in the least when I clambered up and down the ladders to the bookshelves and set about my usual tasks. Naturally I watched him, and saw how he quietly filled page after page with his beautiful, clear handwriting, with scarcely a break. Only seldom was the flow interrupted. Then he would raise his head, staring into emptiness, his eyes never looking out of the window or fixed on any object, but seemingly gazing inwards. Now and then he would mutter a sentence or a few words beneath his breath.

When his fountain pen ran out of ink, I was summoned and each time there was the same complaint, that nowadays you couldn't fill the pen with a glass pipette capped with a little rubber hat, as formerly. Then the pen would stay clean, but these modern pens you had to dip into the ink and dirty them. This much maligned fountain pen is now one of my most treasured possessions.

Very early on Jung had taken to giving the typescripts to his pupils to read before sending them to the printer. All criticisms, all suggestions for changes, cuts or additions were carefully weighed and were generally accepted. But never did Jung react more sharply to misunderstanding or "stupidity" than here. One had to merit his confidence.

We had various places for work. If he wanted to work in the library, I was summoned by two rings on the bell. When I came, he was already seated in his armchair beside the French windows facing south and opening on to a narrow balcony, smoking his morning pipe. I had to take my place in the visitor's chair opposite him. Jung smoked a water-cooled pipe. Taking the bowl and stem apart at short intervals, dipping the stem with its metal tip into the bowl of water placed there for the purpose, pressing down and tapping the tobacco with a small silver tamp flattened at the top, the repeated lightings with the lighter that didn't always want to burn, or with a match, were typical Jungian gestures that accompanied work and conversation. By choice he smoked Granger tobacco. A friend regularly sent him the handsome, dark-blue tins from New York. Now and then Jung prepared his own mixture—a solemn performance at which I had to assist. The mixture was kept in a dark bronze box, which for some unaccountable reason bore the name "Habbakuk."

Jung was no cigarette smoker, but after luncheon he allowed himself a Brazilian cigar, which he would offer also to his friends. I had to see that the supply of cigarillos called "Grüner Heinrich" did not run out. Occasionally he smoked a Brissago,[19] or a strange, snake-like, dark, exotic cigar the name of which I unfortunately never learned. Smoking was one of the pleasures of the day. "A little tobacco assists concentration and contributes to one's peace of mind," was his justification to his doctor.

When the weather was warm and fine, we moved out into the garden. A garden table and two wicker chairs were fetched with Müller's assistance. In summer Jung wore his wide-brimmed panama to protect him from the strong sun. Here there was only one disturbing factor: the ear-splitting din of the squadrons of aircraft that roared across the lake from Dübendorf and vanished behind the mountains. But it was quickly over, and afterwards the silence was all the more

19. A brand of cigar produced in Brissago, Tessin, Switzerland, similar in appearance to the one described.

perceptible. Mostly we sat in the upper part of the garden, near the house. Great blue convolvuli with the beautiful name of "morning-glory" clambered up the east wall and opened out in the sun, a blackbird spread its wings flat on the sunlit lawn or took a bath in the rain water at the bottom of a stone urn atop a high pedestal. Tiny drops of water came spraying out of the urn in a pretty little fountain, while the bathing bird remained hidden. Jung had left the lake end of the garden in its pristine condition–a thick wall of reeds, which became a nesting and breeding place, assiduously and lovingly watched, for swans, ducks, and divers.

When Jung wasn't feeling well enough to go down to the garden, we worked on a large open terrace on the first floor of the house. As he was sensitive to drafts, it had to be protected from the wind before we began work. Wide strips of sailcloth were attached to wires with clothespins or safety pins, a somewhat complicated business at which I was not very adroit, but I could do no better even under Jung's shouted commands. At last everything was ready and fixed to his satisfaction, and the work could begin.

We had been sitting on the terrace shortly before his death, after a stroke had made speaking infinitely difficult for him. Even then he wanted to be told about what was going on in the world, about the letters, people, telephone calls, and gave brief indications of answers, hints of thoughts.

He expected me to have read the letters addressed to him unless the envelope was marked "Personal." Generally, after the dictation, we exchanged a few words about their content and his answer; sometimes this led to a discussion. Once a strange thing happened. Jung broke off dictating a rather inconsequential letter and began to talk. Already after the first words it was as if a curtain had been lifted before the world, as if the whole fabric of creation had become transparent and everything that happened was absolutely understandable. Connections sprang up between the remotest spheres. I cannot express it otherwise than that I shared a moment of illumination. Listening to him, I became motionless and forgot to take the usual notes. When I tried to recall what had happened, on the train from Küsnacht to Zurich, I was dismayed to find that I could no longer do so. Nothing could be called back to memory. So I resolved, feeling very ashamed, to ask Jung to formulate his thoughts again. But the next morning Jung received me with the words: "What was I saying yesterday?" He, too, could remember nothing more, the light was snuffed out. I was very grieved about this, but Jung remained perfectly serene. The time was not ripe, was his explanation.

After our morning work, if the weather was tolerable, Jung would walk a bit in the garden or immerse himself in the *Neue Zürcher Zeitung*. In the evening, after our discussion of the memoirs, or—in former years—after analytical sessions, a couple of small services ushered in his hour of relaxation: a stool was pushed under his feet and a little table with patience cards on it placed on his knees. Jung liked playing patience. He had no compunction, now and then, in an emergency, in helping fate a little by switching the cards around. The game had to come out, dammit! The scandalization of others who caught him out in such unabashed cheating did not disturb him in the slightest, it may even have spiced his enjoyment.

Another source of relaxation was reading detective stories, which lay around everywhere and were piled up in stacks on the topmost floor of the house. He liked English thrillers, but Simenon was his favorite. If the picture on the cover was too lurid, I had to shroud the book in a correct wrapper, so that it might appear innocuously on the slate table in the library. For Jung the figure of the detective was a modern version of the alchemical Mercurius, solver of all riddles, and he was entertained by his heroic deeds. He also enjoyed science fiction.

In winter one had to put on warm clothes because Jung

didn't like the heating to be too strong. On very cold days he wore a brown, fur-lined dressing gown, which lent his tall figure an altogether fabulous dimension. Then came the dark skullcap on the white hair—and, straight out of a fairy tale, the timeless figure of the benign, stern, wise, powerful old man stood before you in the flesh.

Jung worked in the mornings. In the afternoon, generally towards five, he received visitors, who stayed for an hour or two. Patients he saw only by exception. A very regular division of time proved the way of using it to the best. In later years he spent three weeks a month in Küsnacht and one week in Bollingen. This rhythm was less of a strain and suited him. There were also longer holidays, spread out over the year and spent mostly in Bollingen, which more often than not were reserved for writing.

During the Bollingen week I appeared for work every Wednesday, and that was always a great day for me. It was a good half-hour's walk from the Bollingen station to the Tower. On rainy days, with a basket of letters, files, and books on my arm, the road was sometimes hard going, but it seemed to be the custom in those parts for drivers to offer a lift to persons who were no longer young. I remember with particular gratitude the driver of a brewery van, who with the greatest regularity used to catch up with me and take me along with him. Jung was amused by this, especially when I told him of our conversations in Swiss German.

Nobody really knew Jung who had not been with him in Bollingen. Here his feeling for Nature showed itself in a way it couldn't do in Küsnacht. There was nothing romantic or gushing about it; it was a genuine rootedness in his own earth, a communion with the whole countryside. All the peasant work belonged to it, as well as friendship with the free-living animals, the birds and the game. When one summer a ring-snake settled by the shore of the lake, it regularly found its little bowl of milk laid out. But one thing above all gave Bollingen its special quality: silence. Jung was a great one for silence, just as he could on occasion be a torrential talker. The two complemented each other. It was a vital necessity for him to sink himself in profound introversion; this was the fountainhead of helpful and vivifying powers. Creative ideas took shape in the inner and outer stillness. Simple country activities refreshed him, as did also the release from daily duties and etiquette.

Often I could hear from afar the blows of hammer and chisel as Jung worked on a stone, a huge pair of spectacles with sidepieces protecting his eyes from flying splinters. All sorts of motifs had risen out of the stone and forced themselves upon him, to his surprise. In the rough surface of the heavy blocks of hewn stone forming the walls of the Tower he saw figures, just as one does in clouds or inkblots, and their outlines became the ground plan for several carvings. There was the laughing head of the trickster that Jung said looked like Balzac, and a naked female form with arms outstretched towards a mare—he called it Pegasus. There was also a relief of a bear with a ball and one of a snake. Thus these stones lived. Other carvings are mentioned in the memoirs; they were done in a shed near the Tower.

Letters, with their demand for concentration in replying to scientific questions or to unknown persons, were not always welcome in the stillness and serenity of Bollingen, and Jung made no bones about it. One day he announced his distaste with particular emphasis: it had been a black day because he had had to cope with letters! And just as one is apt to identify the messenger with the news he brings, so a few sputterings of his bad temper fell upon me, and my spirits sank. Noticing this, Jung sent me one of those playful signals "sub rosa," which he set great store by and which made him appear in my eyes like a Zen master. He once said he couldn't possibly relate to anyone who didn't understand this game, which the alchemists also knew. So, as I was putting my bits and pieces together for the journey home on that black day—we had been working out of doors by the lake—I saw, to my amazement, Jung bending down and looking at the lake from between his legs, as children do when they want to see the world upside down. He told me to do the same. Though I didn't get what it was all about and was in no mood for practical jokes, I complied and likewise looked at the landscape upside down. Then Jung expatiated on the structure of the eye. Several times he came back to the reasons why the world and things looked better, and were perceived more correctly, if you took the inverse view of them. With that he bade me farewell and vanished into his shed. It took me quite a long time to decipher the message conveyed "sub rosa" by our contortions and to guess the charade—that under these conditions the black day was in fact a bright one!

On Jung's plot of land in Bollingen, just outside the walled enclosure of the Tower, there was a spring which debouched into the lake through several little channels. Generally these were silted up and barely visible. After he bought the land in 1922, he evolved an amusing game he was much addicted to, which consisted in digging new channels for the water to flow along in clear, rippling streams. He used a small narrow shovel with a long shaft—the kind that shepherds in earlier days used for hurling stones at stray animals. Legs apart and bent forward—warmly muffled up in cold weather and with a peaked peasant cap on his head—the old man stood on the patches of earth that rose like islands out of the sand, carefully removing the sand, shovelful by shovelful. He took care to follow the natural gradient so as to dig the right channels for the narrow rivulets and get the water flowing again.

At Bollingen, too, we used to work in the mornings, if possible out of doors, but sometimes by the fireplace in a half-open loggia, and only in cold weather in the study on the upper floor, a very plain, wood-paneled room with a brown tiled stove. A small work table with a paraffin lamp in front of the window, a couch, a bookcase against the wall, and two comfortable armchairs were all the furniture there was. Here Jung did his writing. What at once struck one was the window. The lower half of it was of fluted glass, shutting out the view into the open, of the landscape he loved so much. Not the slightest extraversion, not the smallest distraction was permitted to disturb his concentration, the meditation on his thoughts.

Our work usually ended with feeding the numerous water-birds with leftover scraps of bread. Jung would watch with enjoyment, joining in with loud and stern reproofs when he thought I was distributing the scraps "unfairly" and giving one bird more than the others. Then followed a simple but delicious meal: soup—generally an enriched Knorr or Maggi packet-soup—a dish filled with an abundance of cheeses, butter, bread, and fruit. A cup of coffee and sometimes a liqueur ended the meal. It is well known that Jung was a connoisseur of wine. When I lunched this summer with friends in a hotel in Schmerikon, the neighboring village to Bollingen, our host sat down at the table and told us his memories of the old Professor Jung: how each time he went down to the cellar with him to pick out the wine himself, how a conversation would spring up and, zealously swapping stories, they would sit down on the cellar steps. Unfortunately I no longer remember what wines Jung preferred. But I do know that at times he much enjoyed a simple country wine, and at others a glass of burgundy. Cocktails he detested.

Seldom, or only on special occasions, did I stay in the Tower until evening. At five o'clock the great moment arrived when the preparations for the ample evening meal began. In his old age Jung felt too tired to take an active part, but in earlier years the preparation of a roast on the grill of the fireplace in the loggia or on the kitchen fire was an affair of state at which all who wanted to join in were assigned their roles as assistant cooks and underlings. Every time it had to be confirmed afterwards that the meal had been worth the effort: the roast, with all its finely spiced trimmings, had turned out a culinary masterpiece!

Ordinarily I made my way home in the early afternoon, after Jung had had his siesta. By choice he then set about chopping wood, or stacking it carefully and ingeniously in the wood pile. In earlier years there was work to do in the potato patch or maize field. Sailing, for many years one of his great joys, he had long since had to give up.

Jung died in his house in Küsnacht, amid the great images that filled his soul. As the thought of death had been his familiar for many decades, it did not come as an enemy, although he was familiar also with the pain caused by the finiteness of life. He gave expression to it in a letter:

> The spectacle of eternal nature makes me painfully aware of my weakness and perishability, and I find no joy in imagining an equanimity *in conspectu mortis*. As I once dreamt, my will to live is a glowing daimon, who sometimes makes the consciousness of my mortality hellish difficult for me. One can, at most, save face like the unjust steward, and then not always, so that my lord wouldn't find even that much to commend. But the daimon recks nothing of that, for life, at the core, is steel on stone.

Jung wrote the letter in May 1953, eight years before his death. It does not convey his basic attitude, but it does reflect the mood of a man approaching the end of his life.

Subsequently it turned out that Jung's dying and his death

were "known" by friends and acquaintances both near and far, that the unconscious had announced the event in dreams before the news spread round the world. The dreams have been collected. A couple of hours after his death there was a violent thunderstorm, and lightning struck a tall poplar in the garden beside the lake, where he was accustomed to sitting. The lightning sizzled along the trunk into the ground, displacing the heavy stones of a low parapet. From the open wound it had burned into the bark I cut out a strip of bast. Then the gardener stopped up the wound with pitch, and the tree is still alive today.

One autumn morning in Bollingen, Jung made me promise to give clear and forthright answers about his life, his personality, and his thoughts when he was no longer there. The brief conversation was sober, almost casual; Jung was no friend of big words. For a long time I hesitated to tell of Jung the man, because this is far more difficult than giving an account of his work and letting his personality shine forth from behind his ideas.

The huge tree of his spirit has sunk roots deep into the earth. Its crown is visible far and wide; it is the work he left to posterity. Of the roots, of the repose in nature, little is known. His personality had infinitely many facets, and everyone knew only the side that was turned towards him. Thus, in my short account, I can throw only a few sidelights on the man as I saw him, and as he appeared to me in the daily round of the last years of his life.

V.

The Creative Phases in Jung's Life

At the age of seventy Jung responded in a letter to the question of phases in the life of a man: "It is exceedingly difficult to write anything definite or descriptive about the progression of psychological states. It always seemed to me as if the real milestones were certain symbolic events characterized by a strong emotional tone."[1] A presentation of the creative phases in Jung's life will therefore deal with such milestones, reporting those events which were marked by a strong emotional tone, then briefly indicating the resultant changes in his intellectual outlook or his attitude toward life.

The work of a creative person has a long history. It does not step into the light of day suddenly, without motivation; inner, and sometimes also outer, events prepare its emergence long beforehand. The stream of creativity digs its bed underground for long stretches of the way and then quite unpredictably breaks through to the surface. Usually the underground course cannot be traced afterwards, or only by intuition, for the necessary information is lacking. With Jung it is different.

1. The letter was written in English (28 August 1945); the translation from Aniela Jaffé's German version, which helps understand its meaning, would read: "It is extraordinarily difficult to say anything definite about the sequence of psychic stages, or to describe them. Certain symbolic events, characterized by a strong emotional tone, appeared to me always as real milestones."

In his memoirs he describes early childhood experiences, dreams, unusual games, frightening experiences; these can be understood as preparations for the later creative phases of his life. They are the first indications of the genius that was struggling to incarnate itself in him, and they reveal the inner law that shaped his destiny. Yet, until the decisive moment, it remains an unanswerable question whether the breakthrough will succeed or not, whether the man will withstand the onslaught of creative genius or break under it.

I want to cite one of Jung's childhood dreams because it allows a glimpse of the hidden daimon of creativity and presages a destiny. It occurs in the fourth or fifth year of his life, a phase which, like puberty, middle life, and the time before death, is marked by intense activity of the unconscious and an increased number of "big" dreams.

The boy discovers a hole in the ground with steps leading downward into the depths. Hesitantly and afraid he goes down and comes to a green curtain which blocks his view. He is curious and pushes it aside, and behind it finds a wonderful golden throne at the end of a long room. On the throne sits a gigantic thing like a tree trunk, reaching nearly to the ceiling. It consists of skin and living flesh and has a cone-shaped head but no face or hair. On its skull is a single eye that gazes steadily upward. Around its head is a glow of light that illuminates the entire room. The boy has the feeling that "this thing" is about to descend from the throne and crawl toward him. He is paralyzed with terror. "At that moment I heard from outside and above me my mother's voice. She called out, 'Yes, just look at him. That is the man-eater!' That intensified my terror still more, and I awoke sweating and scared to death."[2]

2. *Memories, Dreams, Reflections*, recorded and edited by Aniela Jaffé, translated by Richard and Clara Winston (New York, 1961), pp. 11 ff. Referred to in the text as "memoirs" and in the notes hereafter as *Memories*.

The underground setting of the dream points to an event that is still completely unconscious. Power, majesty, and numinosity all reside in this phallic daimon, a *tremendum* the very sight of which paralyzes the child with terror. But this dream image also has an entirely different, very positive aspect: the shape of the daimon, as also the light radiating from it and the upward-gazing eye,[3] characterizes it as a living, creative, and perceiving spirit dwelling in the dark recesses of the psyche.

The dream image of the mother is equally ambivalent. She herself remains invisible; only her voice is heard, inviting the boy to observe the creature more closely. But she takes back the invitation, as though mockingly, by pointing out its murderous qualities, and actually tempts the boy to flee. Her call seems to have the secret design of preventing her son's fateful encounter with the daimon. Were the boy to yield to this maternal temptation, a perilous venture would not be undertaken, a destiny go unfulfilled. Thus the kind, understanding, and adored mother presents as deadly a danger as her hostile counterpart. Moreover, we know from the laws of dream events that the phallic daimon shows itself so threatening and terrifying only because it is denied, and not the other way round. Seen in the light of depth psychology, a man's destiny is always shaped at the point where his fear lies.

Jung recalls in his memoirs that he experienced the phallic figure as a "subterranean God 'not to be named'," who appeared to him throughout his youth as the antagonist of the trusted, bright Lord Jesus. It was "an unsought-after, frightful revelation," an "initiation into the realm of darkness." Jung concludes his description of this dream: "My intellectual life had its unconscious beginnings at that time." In point of fact, the ambiguity of both dream figures and the ten-

3. Etymologically, "phallus" is related to the Greek word meaning "shining," "brilliant."

sion between them express the fundamental motif of his work: man suspended between the opposites. The boy experienced the opposites as Christ/Lucifer, light/darkness, which means also good/evil or conscious/unconscious.

A few years later the dream came true: Jung fell into a neurotic conflict between creativity and inertia. We shall return to this point later. One can say, however, from a survey of his development as a whole, that the ithyphallic light-giving daimon, this symbol of a spiritual impulse slumbering in the unconscious of the child, completely mastered him after he had overcome the neurotic crisis, that everything else had to retreat before its advance, and that Jung survived because he obeyed. At the age of eighty-two he wrote:

> I have had much trouble getting along with my ideas. There was a daimon in me, and in the end its presence proved decisive. It overpowered me. . . . I had to obey an inner law which was imposed on me and left me no freedom of choice. . . . A creative person has little power over his own life. He is not free. He is captive and driven by his daimon. . . . This lack of freedom has been a great sorrow to me.[4]

From the "initiation into the realm of darkness" it would appear to have been decreed by fate that Jung's creative impulse should tend toward the negative pole of the psychic opposites. From the beginning the content of his research and writing is characterized by a preponderance of the dark aspects of the psyche. But this does not mean world-negation or nihilism, for he always remembered the vision of light in the darkness which he saw for the first time in his childhood dream. He wanted to illuminate the dark, unknown, rejected side of the psyche. In the imagery of a different culture, one could say that he was drawn to the core of light in Yin and the core of darkness in Yang.

4. *Memories*, pp. 356–57.

For a child raised in the strictly Christian milieu of a parsonage, the terrifying dream figure was, quite literally, a phenomenon and wholly unique. It had no outside model. The sensitive boy perceived it as a giant arising out of the depths of the psyche. Jung was still haunted by this image in later years, so much so that it played a part in his discovery of the archetypes. Looking back, he describes his childhood experiences, among them this dream, as primordial experiences, revelations of a spirit buried in the unconscious, or as invasions from the unconscious into his life. Even as a boy he had been profoundly impressed by the strangeness of their contents. Under the influence of their numinosity he reacted with what one might call a natural, religious instinct. He kept them a closely guarded secret for many years, speaking about them to no one and creating his own taboos.

One may readily understand that a child who is haunted by such dream images—or to whom the grace of such an inner vision is granted—can enter into the reality of this world only with the greatest effort. In approximately the same period as this dream there was an unconscious attempt at suicide: the boy suddenly fell down on a bridge (crossing the Rhine at Laufen near his parents' house), slid under the railing, and was caught just in time by the maid who hauled him back to safety. Jung speaks of his "fatal resistance to life in this world." But in the background was a fatal resistance to the dark daimon under whose sign his life in this world was meant to run its course, an unconscious shrinking back before the demands of his own creativity. This regressive tendency went hand in hand with an equally unconscious longing for security in the mother, whose ambiguous words had given that dream its peculiarly uncanny character.

When Jung was twelve years old, the "fatal resistance to life in this world" obtruded once more and led to a neurosis. He suffered from more or less genuine fainting spells and stayed out of school for a half year or more. "I frittered away my time with loafing, collecting, reading, and playing. But I did not feel any happier for it; I had the obscure feeling that I was fleeing from myself."[5]

Significantly enough, it was the voice of his father that finally called Jung to reality when he overheard his father telling a friend with great concern of his son's condition. In a flash the boy realized the danger of his dreamy, idle life; from then on he fought with great resolution against his laziness and fainting spells. In a short time he overcame both. One might speak here of a first victory over the mother, though he himself called it a "defeat." "A few weeks later I returned to school, and never suffered another attack. The whole bag of tricks was over and done with! That was when I learned what a neurosis is."[6] The result of his ordeal was "a studied punctiliousness and unusual diligence. Those days saw the beginnings of my conscientiousness, practised not for the sake of appearances, so that I would amount to something, but for my own sake."[7] This was Jung's tribute to the father's world, and right into old age it remained the sine qua non of his research and attitude toward life. At the age of seventy-six he wrote in a letter in English: "For the time being I am undergoing the curse of letter-writing. Only through submission to detestable duties can one gain a certain feeling of liberation which induces a creative mood. In the long run one cannot steal creation."

After the "defeat" of the neurosis, Jung's life ran on for quite a while without any special difficulties. The longing for security and the dangerous inertia were vanquished, the gate to the underworld had closed, and therewith the preparatory phase of his creativity came to an end. The following years

5. Ibid., p. 31.
6. Ibid., pp. 30–32.
7. Ibid., p. 32.

are filled with work, friendship, and the joy of living as schoolboy, student, and young psychiatrist. In 1903, at the age of twenty-eight, he married Emma Rauschenbach, and in 1906 moved into his own house in Küsnacht near Zürich.

The dissertation, "On the Psychology and Pathology of So-Called Occult Phenomena" (1902), dedicated to his fiancée and written at the suggestion of Eugen Bleuler, his chief, formed the prelude to the first creative period. Based upon carefully observed experimental séances with his mediumistically gifted cousin, it is an exposition and psychological interpretation of her trance utterances. Jung's interest and scientific curiosity were drawn even in those early days to observable facts, and facts remained the basis of his research to the end of his life. He laid great stress on being understood as an empiricist. In the later creative phases, however, he gave up experimentation, and descriptive studies of case material took second place and finally were dropped altogether. Instead of clinical histories of individuals and their fates, we find documents from the history of the human mind: myths, fairy tales, poetry, and religious, mystical, and heretical sayings, as well as a mass of alchemical material. The personal was superseded by the impersonal, and dreams in turn came to be considered more for their archetypal content than for their personal meaning. (In his psychotherapeutic and analytical practice, the emphasis was of course distributed differently, so that the personal element was given due weight.)

In this first creative phase Jung's interest was turned more to the dark aspects of the psyche: the realm of the occult, the unconscious background and its feeling-toned complexes, which he discovered by means of the association experiments, and above all, the chaotic world of the insane. In "The Psychology of Dementia Praecox" (1907) and "The Content of the Psychoses" (1908), he struggled to understand the statements and symptoms of the mentally ill, which had until then been dismissed as nonsense, and to find an orderly structure in psychic chaos. Against every psychiatric opinion of the day, he succeeded in reaching his goal by dint of infinite patience, perseverance, and empathy. In several cases he even managed to cure psychotic patients with the help of psychotherapy, to reintegrate them into the world of work and human relationship, something that up to that time was unthinkable. The discovery of archaic contents in the unconscious, which by invading a too weak or too narrow consciousness can work destruction and lead to a psychosis, as also the irrefutable proof of feeling-toned complexes, heralded Jung's later theory of archetypes. We can draw a straight line from his doctoral dissertation on occult phenomena, over various stations of his work, to the exposition of the principle of synchronicity half a century later. The first creative period was in every respect a foundation for the development of his later work and bore the seeds of fruitful developments to come.

The encounter with Freud marked the high point and conclusion of this first period.[8] Their acquaintance began in 1906 with an exchange of letters. Freud returned thanks for Jung's *Studies in Word Association*, which he had received from Jung as a gift but had already bought and read beforehand. Freud sent Jung his *Sammlung kleiner Schriften zur Neurosenlehre*. Their first meeting took place one year later, in 1907. Jung met in Freud an older, more experienced man who was traveling the same road as he was, for Freud too was intent on opening up the hidden recesses of the psyche. For the first time Jung had encountered a congenial personality, and he was overjoyed to feel understood and supported in his scientific investigations. It need hardly be said that the discussion quickly turned to psychoanalysis. Nineteen years his senior, Freud inevitably became for Jung a father-figure to whose scientific authority he sought for a long time to submit him-

8. Cf. the chapter "Sigmund Freud" in *Memories*.

self as a pupil and apprentice. Early in 1909 he wrote to Freud: "The high degree of assurance and composure that distinguish you is not yet mine generally speaking. . . . Countless things that are commonplaces for you are still brand new experiences for me, which I have to relive afterwards until they tear me to pieces." On his side Freud acknowledged Jung's great gifts and was stirred by the human warmth of his personality. In Jung he believed he had found his long-sought spiritual son and successor. In this archetypal father-son situation lay the fruitfulness of their relationship—and also, as will be shown, the seed of its demise.

So far as creative work goes, the period of collaboration with Freud was not especially productive for Jung.[9] A great deal of energy was taken up with mundane affairs—congresses, the founding and editing of the *Jahrbuch für psychoanalytische und psychotherapeutische Forschungen*, and most of all with Jung's militant defense, in his lectures and writings, of Freud's psychoanalysis, then under heavy attack from all sides. It was a period of learning and assimilation on the one hand and of growing extraversion on the other. True introvert that he was, Jung was enjoying the positive side of extraversion—travel and success—now for once in full measure. In September 1909 he wrote to his wife from Clark University, where he had been invited with Freud and where he delivered lectures on the association experiment: "We are the men of the day over here. It is very good to be able to enjoy this side a bit. I feel that my libido is enjoying it in full measure."[10]

Countless reasons have been advanced to explain the break between Jung and Freud. In the view of analytical psychology

9. Besides the works on the association experiment he wrote "Psychic Conflicts in a Child" (1910), "A Contribution to the Psychology of Rumor" (1910–11), "The Significance of the Father in the Destiny of the Individual" (1909), and "The Theory of Psychoanalysis" (1913).

10. Cf. *Memories*, pp. 365 ff.

they are principally: Freud's one-sided emphasis on the sexual factor, his rejection of religion, his reductive causalistic thinking, his unwillingness to accept Jung's new and divergent ideas, as well as various human and personal weaknesses. All these reasons are valid. Nevertheless, they seem to me to pale before one primary fact: Freud, like Jung, was caught by the creative daimon, and each had to follow his own law. Even though both men were intent on illuminating the dark background of the psyche, their visions were so different that agreement was impossible in the long run and their separation inevitable. Moreover, Freud had already found his own way, while Jung, who was thirty-two years old when they first met, still stood on the threshold of his most creative period. To be sure, he had won an international reputation as a medical pioneer through his work on dementia praecox and the association experiment even before his collaboration with Freud, but in order to learn from the older and more experienced man he submitted to his authority longer than inner necessity demanded. Freud on his side made the mistake of plying Jung with his paternal demands and moreover named him his successor or, as he himself said, the "crown prince." Jung resisted this from the beginning. In the last analysis, neither of them bore in mind that the creative person must serve his own daimon and may not bind himself to anyone or anything outside his own life's task. The resentment that continued to smolder on both sides right up to their deaths probably had its roots in their failure to observe this psychological law.

Jung's most important work from this encounter with Freud is his *Symbols of Transformation*.[11] It develops ideas that diverged from Freud's views and forms the conclusion of this period. The preparations for it reach back to 1909 when Jung

11. It appeared in two parts in the *Jahrbuch für psychoanalytische und psychopathologische Forschungen*, 1911 and 1912, and at the same time as a book published by Deuticke Verlag, Leipzig.

took up once more, after years of neglect, his studies of mythology and the history of religion. He was deeply impressed but felt incapable of organizing the mass of material until by chance there fell into his hands the fantasy series of an unknown young American woman, a pre-psychotic, whose fantasies stemmed directly from the unconscious. The main content of the series had to do with the hero and his confrontation with the mother. Attempting to interpret the images, Jung discovered to his amazement identical or analogous motifs to those he had found in classical mythology. This astonishing fact could not be explained by Freud's view of the unconscious as the receptacle of repressed contents. Much more, it confirmed Jung's long-guarded suspicion that behind the repressed contents lay a still deeper layer of the unconscious whose content consisted of innate, structural forms that endured beyond space and time. Later (in 1917) he described this layer as the collective unconscious and the layer of repressed and forgotten contents as the personal unconscious.

The real divergence between Jung's standpoint and Freud's first came to light in the theme of mother-son incest. Jung dealt with it in the last chapter of *Symbols of Transformation*, entitled "The Sacrifice." In his memoirs he tells of his apprehension that Freud would never be able to accept his interpretation of incest; he had the intuition that this chapter would also mean the sacrifice of his friendship with Freud.

Freud understood the incest motif in dreams, fantasies, myths, and in the neurotic son's mother complex literally and personally, i.e., in the sexual sense. Jung did not exclude this possibility, but far more important for him was the symbolic meaning of incest. The mother is not only the material source of mankind's existence but also the psychic source; insofar as consciousness has developed gradually out of the unconscious and continues to do so over and over again, the unconscious is, figuratively speaking, the psycho-spiritual mother. When union or "incest" with the mother occurs in dreams or myths, it signifies a sinking of consciousness into the unconscious, a primordial danger to mankind. For youth this psychic incest expresses persistence in the security of the mother, in a state of twilight bliss and effortless ease. It is the danger which was boded forth in Jung's childhood dream and in due course laid him low with his childhood neurosis.

Psychic incest can be overcome only at the price of a sacrifice. It is the sacrifice of the regressive libido, which tugs backwards toward the mother-child situation; the wish for perpetual security in the mother must be given up. The fatal inertia must surrender fully to the world's demands and retreat before the challenges and perils of life in the world, for "the sacrifice of the libido that strives back to the past necessarily results in the creation of the world."[12]

In the first half of life the libido flows naturally outwards into the world. A person's life is arrested or destroyed if he does not follow the gradient but succumbs to the regressive longing for the mother. After middle life, however, the symbolic meaning of psychic incest changes. When old age and death begin to cast their shadows, other psychological necessities are constellated which differ from those of the expansive phase of youth. Now the libido presses naturally inwards to the unconscious, this time not as a flight from life into effortless security but out of longing for an eternal reality behind everyday, time-bound reality, in other words, out of desire for spiritual transformation in rebirth. Jesus' answer to Nicodemus's question expresses this aspect of incest: "'How can a man be born when he is old? Can he enter a second time into his mother's womb and be born?' Jesus answered, 'Truly, truly, I say to you, unless one is born of water and the Spirit, he cannot enter the kingdom of God'" (John 3:4–5, RSV).

12. C. G. Jung, *Collected Works* (*CW*) 5, §646.

The way into one's own depths, the Faustian descent to the Mothers, means for the mature person no less hazardous an undertaking and demands no less a sacrifice of security than does the severance from the mother and the advance into the world during youth. Everything depends on the aging person's not letting himself be overpowered by the regressive longing, on the depths not engulfing him, and on himself undertaking the descent consciously and freely. "And let those who go down the sunset way do so with open eyes, for it is a sacrifice which daunts even the gods."[13]

Jung knew the danger of psychic mother-incest from his childhood experiences. Still in the future, however, was the voluntary descent into the mother, and it became one of the most meaningful experiences for his creative development. Of this we shall have more to say later. For the present it was a matter of proceeding intellectually on his own toward a new interpretation of the incest problem.

Jung's symbolic interpretation of incest and Freud's personalistic-sexual one were irreconcilable. Although this difference resulted partly from intellectual disagreements, it was ultimately grounded in the psychological nature of the two men. Jung had an intense, lifelong relation to the mother, that is, to the collective unconscious, its irrational imagery and symbolism. He himself spoke of his permeability to the psychic background. Occasionally he referred to his mother complex in a negative way, calling it a fascination with the "Eternal Feminine," but this turned out to be the prerequisite for his creative work. Freud's nature and creative destiny were quite different. In his *Interpretation of Dreams,* he reports a nightmare from his seventh or eighth year in which his beloved mother, dead, is carried into a room by two or three persons with birds' beaks. The bird-people remind him of an Egyptian tomb relief. The boy awakens crying and screaming.

13. Ibid. §553.

As was the case with Jung's childhood dream, this solemn, frightening image presages a destiny. The pall-bearers are related to the bird-headed Horus, and because of the solar quality of this God they must be governed by the realm of daylight, by logos and reason. They are the ones who carry the mother to the grave. Clearly, then, the spiritual destiny, the creative work of a man who as a child comes upon such a powerful dream image of his mother's death, cannot be determined by the matriarchal feminine but will stand under the sign of the opposite spiritual pole, the masculine paternal logos.[14] The lucid scientific spirit which permeates Freud's thinking and writing and the logic of his scientific deductions receive their support from this reservoir of his being.

Jung placed enormous importance on Freud's understanding of his thought, and in his letters he took great pains to make himself understood. But Freud's replies bespeak an almost tragic inability to follow him.[15] These letters, exchanged between 1911 and 1912, already constitute the last act of the drama; finally neither Freud's expressions of mistrust nor Jung's incivilities made any further difference. They were merely external occasions for signaling the break-up of the friendship.

After his separation from Freud, nearly all of Jung's former friends and acquaintances fell away from him. In addition to the pain of losing his connection with Freud, Jung suffered a sense of isolation. He never overcame completely his resentment against Freud—this remained on both sides. Neverthe-

14. E. F. Horine, "Anima and Eros Aspects in some Dreams of Sigmund Freud," unpublished dissertation, C. G. Jung Institute-Zürich, 1970.

15. Freud expressed himself in very sharp words on the subject of Jung and his thought, especially on the symbolic understanding of incest, in his "On the History of the Psychoanalytic Movement," 1914 (*Standard Edition*, vol. 14). Ernest Jones characterized his comments as "polemical," Sandor Ferenczi as "a bomb."

less, he was conscious of Freud's intellectual greatness, and he never forgot what his own creative work owed to Freud. At the age of eighty-two Jung wrote in a letter:

> Despite the blatant misjudgment I have suffered at Freud's hands, I cannot fail to recognize, even in the teeth of my resentment, his significance as a critic of culture and pioneer in the field of psychology. A true assessment of Freud's achievement would take us into areas of the mind that concern not only Jews but Europeans in general, areas that I have sought to illuminate in my works. Without Freud's 'psychoanalysis' I wouldn't have had a clue.

When Jung broke with Freud he was thirty-seven years old. Referring to his book *Symbols of Transformation*, he later admitted in a letter, almost apologetically, that he had found his own thoughts only at the end of his fourth decade. He liked to attribute this to the planet Saturn, which stood in the first house of his horoscope and, according to the ancient astrological rule, exerts a powerful, restricting influence.

One might have expected a phase of intense intellectual activity following his liberation from Freud's paternal authority. This was not the case. A profound uncertainty about his own creative path overcame Jung. He states in his memoirs: "After the parting of ways with Freud, a period of uncertainty began for me. It would be no exaggeration to call it a state of disorientation. I felt totally suspended in mid-air, for I had not yet found my own footing."[16] His creative powers, it seemed, had deserted him. It appears at first glance absurd to trace this standstill to the revolutionary, pioneering thoughts on the hero and his confrontation with the mother, which were the primary themes of *Symbols of Transformation*. But those thoughts were only theoretical and, as every psychologist knows, the day is not carried by theory. Recalling his own

16. *Memories*, p. 170.

experience, Jung wrote to Erich Neumann: "In the case of bad books, it is enough that they get written. Good books, however, want to realize themselves and begin to pose questions which one would rather leave others to answer" (28 February 1952). In his memoirs he says: "I had wanted to go on with the scientific analysis of myths which I had begun in *Symbols of Transformation*. That was still my goal—but I must not think of that! I was being compelled to go through the process of the unconscious. I had to let myself be carried along by the current, without a notion of where it would lead me."[17]

Disoriented and perplexed by this blockage of the creative process, Jung felt his libido pulling back more and more from the world and turning within. A series of dreams strengthened the introversive tendency, and all attempts at overcoming the disturbance by rational means and of fighting against the regressive trend came to nothing. In this perilous situation he decided to yield to the urge and listen to what was trying to get at him from within. Thus began his voluntary descent into the Realm of the Mothers.

The first thing to come up was a childhood memory: he saw himself playing passionately with building blocks. Accompanying this image was the feeling, actually a conviction, that the boy possessed the creative life which had slipped away from him.[18] He drew the conclusion:

> . . . I had no choice but to return to it and take up once more that child's life with his childish games. This moment was a turning point in my fate, but I gave in only after endless resistance and with a sense of resignation. For it was a painfully humiliating experience to realize that there was nothing to be done except play childish games.[19]

17. Ibid., p. 196.
18. Ibid., p. 174.
19. Ibid.

So as not to falsify the picture one must add that, although Jung certainly did spend some time playing with building blocks, during this long regressive period, stretching out over nearly six years (until 1918), he lived a normal middle-class life as psychiatrist and psychotherapist with a large international practice, and his family never had to suffer on account of his preoccupation. During the First World War he acted as a health commissioner, and in 1918 he became commandant of the interned British prisoners of war at Château d'Oex, for which he received a citation from the British. Jung paid his tribute to the world in full measure. Seen from the outside, his descent into the depths and confrontation with the unconscious lay on the periphery of his life; but seen from within they stood at the very center. It is characteristic that while commandant at Château d'Oex he reached decisive insights which initiated a new creative phase. Of that I shall have more to say later.

The building game was only a prelude, a *rite d'entré*. It released a stream of fantasies and had also a calming effect on the emotions bound up with these inner images. Jung carefully wrote down all his fantasies and thoughts during this period, and in the course of years there grew up a voluminous manuscript of approximately six hundred typewritten pages. An account of the genesis of this manuscript—the "Red Book"[20]—is given in the memoirs, together with a summary of the initial series of fantasies.[21] Because of its private nature, however, its publication is proscribed. Jung placed a copy of the manuscript at my disposal with permission to quote from it as occasion arose. I am using this permission here for the first time.

For the purpose of understanding Jung's creative phases the first two chapters are the most revealing, for they furnish an insight into the initial conflict which set off the regression of

20. *Memories*, p. 188 & n. 6.
21. Ibid., pp. 181 ff.

libido. They contain also a sharp critique of the preceding creative period.

The manuscript begins by counterposing a "spirit of the times" and a spirit who "rules over the depths of everything in the present."

> Filled with human pride and blinded by the presumptuous spirit of the times, I long sought to hold that other spirit away from me. But I did not pause to consider that the spirit of the depths from time immemorial and for all time to come possessed a greater power than the spirit of the times, who changes with the generations and withers with the flowers of summer. . . . The spirit of the depths took my understanding and all my knowledge and placed them at the service of the inexplicable and the paradoxical, or rather what must appear so to the people of these times. He robbed me of power to speak and write of anything that was not in his service, namely in the service of fusing together sense and nonsense. . . . By my fortieth year I had achieved everything I had wished for as a child. I had gained fame, power, wealth, knowledge, and the best human fortune. Then my desire for increasing these good things ceased, the desire retreated. . . . I felt the spirit of the depths, but I did not understand him.

Above the second chapter Jung wrote: "The Rediscovery of the Soul." There we find the following:

> I have returned, I am once again there—
> I am with you—after long years of long wandering
> I have come again to you.
> Should I tell you everything I have seen, experienced, drunk into myself?
> Or don't you want to hear of all the noise of life and the world?
> But one thing you must know, one thing I have learnt, that one must live this life.
> This life is the way, the longest sought after, the way to the incomprehensible, which we call divine.
> There is no other way.
> All other ways are false paths.

> I found the right way, it led me to you, to
> my soul.
> I return, tempered and purified.
>
> Then I was still utterly engrossed in the spirit of the times and thought differently of the human soul.
>
> I thought and spoke much about the soul; I knew many learned words about the soul; I judged it and made a scientific object of it.
>
> I did not consider that the soul cannot be the object of my judgment and knowledge. Much more are my judgment and knowledge the object of my soul.
>
> Therefore the spirit of the depths pressed me to speak to my soul, to call upon it as a living and independent being whose re-discovery means good fortune for me. I had to become aware that I had lost my soul, or rather that I had lost myself from my soul, for many years.
>
> The spirit of the depths sees the soul as an independent, living being, and therewith contradicts the spirit of the times for whom the soul is something dependent on the person, which lets itself be ordered and judged, that is, a thing whose range we can grasp.
>
> Before the spirit of the depths this thought is presumption and arrogance. Therefore the joy of my re-discovery was a humble one. . . . Without the soul there is no way out of this time.

The "spirit of the depths" opens up the long series of images which emerge from the unconscious. Thus the daimon returns a generation later and in changed form, the daimon who once appeared in a childhood dream as a compensatory god to the conscious world and forecast a destiny. His first appearance frightened the child, and the mother voiced a warning; now Jung says, "I long sought to hold that other spirit away from me." But because the preceding period had been lived and lived fully, he had now in middle life reached the point where the enantiodromia could begin and the libido which had been turned to the world turned back within.

The realization, formulated here for the first time, that the soul cannot be the object of judgment and knowledge, but that judgment and knowledge are the object of the soul, contains one of the most essential thoughts of Jung's later work. The epistemological insight that all knowledge rests on human experience and is conditioned by the human being, that "the 'giver' of all 'given' things dwells within us,"[22] became a refrain, returning again and again in nearly all the later writings. This repeated emphasis was necessary because it involves a perception that does not easily penetrate naive feeling. Natural feeling clings tenaciously, often incorrigibly, to the objectivity of what is perceived, thought, revealed. Thus Jung stirred up vigorous opposition when he asserted that the knowledge of God "proceeds from the nature of the soul," i.e., is knowledge of a God-image in the human soul, though this asserts nothing about the existence and being of God himself. The psychically conditioned nature of all knowing, experiencing, and perceiving, even of all revelation, essentially characterized Jung's image of man and his place in the inner and outer cosmos.

Following the two introductory chapters from which I have quoted, we find descriptions of the actual fantasies. Having yielded to the pull of the unconscious and let himself fall into the depths, Jung experienced a superabundance of inner figures. It amounted to an individual revelation that went on for several years. He himself spoke of a primordial experience. But he did not let matters rest there, for this subjective experience later became the most powerful challenge for his creative scientific work.

> All my works, all my creative activity, has come [*sic*] from those initial fantasies and dreams. . . . Everything that I accomplished in later life was already contained in them, although at first only in the form of emotions and images.[23]
>
> It all began then; the later details are only supplements and

22. Cf. "Psychological Commentary on *The Tibetan Book of the Dead,*" *CW* 11, §841.
23. *Memories*, p. 192.

> clarifications of the material that burst forth from the unconscious, and at first swamped me. It was the *prima materia* for a lifetime's work.[24]

Jung integrated this primordial experience, which could also be described as a mystical experience or gnosis, into the thinking of his time through his scientific work. In this intellectual task the spirit of the depths bound itself to the spirit of the times, and in the union of the seemingly irreconcilable opposites of inner and outer worlds, unconscious and conscious, lay his healing. It was a victory over the danger of sinking into the unconscious; seen in the light of his fundamental problem, it was the victory over the mother.

Jung came forth from his night-sea-journey a transformed man. He had overcome the mother, and his own spirit now bore the marks of the maternal feminine, a receptive and fruitful womb which could recast the unknown and strange into familiar forms.[25]

Integration of the maternal also altered his "soul-image," the anima. A younger anima figure emerged in place of a mother-anima. At that time he met Toni Wolff, who became his helper in the intellectual penetration of the world of psychic images and remained his helper until her death in 1953. Alchemically, she was his "soror mystica."

Psychotherapy was to benefit from Jung's "experiment" with the unconscious, for from it he developed the method of "active imagination" as a form of psychological meditation and as an aid in bringing to consciousness unconscious contents. Later he compared the world of images which had emerged into the light, this treasure-house of feelings and emotions, to the world opened up by psychedelic drugs. But while the products of active imagination must be consciously

24. Ibid., p. 199.
25. With these words Jung characterized his friend Richard Wilhelm. Cf. "Richard Wilhelm: In Memoriam," *CW* 15, §76.

worked for and are for that reason in accord with the individual's spiritual development, the magic world of drug experience comes as an unearned gift, with the result that the unconscious grows more and more remorseless in its demands and the task of assimilating its contents more difficult than ever.

Right at the beginning of the regressive phase, Jung saw himself faced with the choice between pursuing his promising academic career at the university or continuing his experiment at "having it out" with the unconscious. Although the choice was not easy for him, he sacrificed his professional career.[26] But he built on what he himself formulated as "more important *sub specie aeternitas*."[27] This decision was like a vow, and he kept it to the death. He says in the memoirs: "It was then that I ceased to belong to myself alone, ceased to have the right to do so. From then on, my life belonged to the generality."[28] In the visions and fantasies a message had come to him as though from a superior power, which was meant not only for himself but also for his fellow men. The carrying out of his life's task required his whole energy and complete submission to the transpersonal.

After about four years the regression gradually subsided. It was in 1916 that Jung felt the first impulse to give it form. As a result he produced the "Septem Sermones ad Mortuos," a kind of poem in Gnostic style, which differs from the other fantasies by its concentrated language and content. It summarizes the most essential ideas in his fantasies and is therefore both a review of the phase of introversion now drawing to an end and a preview of work to come.

Jung's lecture (in French) "The Structure of the Unconscious" also marks 1916 as an important year. In it he tried

26. *Memories*, p. 194.
27. Ibid.
28. *Memories*, p. 192.

for the first time to present, however sketchily, his experiences in scientific form; twelve years later he reworked the lecture into his seminal essay "The Relations between the Ego and the Unconscious."[29]

This most remarkable and critical phase of regression came to a definite end in 1918. It was the concept of individuation, already sketched out in "Septem Sermones," that gave him relief, peace of mind, and the will to return to the world of scientific research; for the individuation process brings about the conjunction of opposites for which Jung had struggled during the preceding years. Individuation means the progressive integration of the timeless background; we might even say of the unconscious self in the time- and space-bound individual. The unique personality becomes one of the myriad facets, unique in itself, of the primordial, unknown and unknowable reality and crystallizes its own being in this way.

Forming the conclusion of the fantasies is the insight that this process of individuation is not linear; it circumambulates its goal—wholeness—in an endless approximation. The symbol of this way is the circle, or mandala, which at the same time represents the goal, wholeness itself. Jung came to this realization during his period of military service at Château d'Oex. In the memoirs he notes: "It became increasingly plain to me that the mandala is the center. It is the exponent of all paths. It is the path to the center, to individuation."[30] It was only after a decade of intensive research and testing that Jung published these ideas; he did so in a book, written jointly with Richard Wilhelm, on the Chinese alchemical Taoist

29. In 1916 he also wrote "The Psychology of the Unconscious Processes" (later reworked and expanded into "On the Psychology of the Unconscious," *CW* 7) and "The Transcendent Function" (*CW* 8), which was published for the first time in 1957. Cf. R. F. C. Hull, "A Prefatory Note to Two Posthumous Papers of C. G. Jung," *Spring 1970.*

30. *Memories,* p. 196.

text *The Secret of the Golden Flower*. This long hesitation is characteristic and indicates his cautious, painstaking method of working. As much as he loved to give free rein to his thoughts and intuitions—in conversation for example (he called this "mythologizing")—his hypotheses had to be thoroughly supported by facts before he presented them to the world.

The Secret of the Golden Flower was the first alchemical text to come to Jung's attention. As he worked on his "European Commentary," the experience he had already had in his mythological studies was repeated and deepened: he came upon the description of forms and images which had confronted him in his own fantasies. What impressed him most was the primary role of the mandala in Chinese alchemy, not only in the form of the golden flower itself but also as the image of circling round the center, or in the "circulation of the light." This circulation indicates that the process of self-becoming has begun; now Tao takes the lead. Similarly Jung had experienced circumambulation as a symbol of individuation, in which the self takes the lead. The discovery of this analogy pointed the way ahead. Looking back, Jung writes in his memoirs: "That was the first event that broke through my isolation. I became aware of an affinity; I could establish ties with something and someone."[31] Now he knew where he had to set to work scientifically in order to find the historical antecedents of his personal experiences: it was alchemy.[32] The oppressive feeling of having been stuck all these years in an inaccessible spiritual world, cut off from the thinking of other people, gradually ebbed away and finally disappeared. At the same time he had the good fortune of having found in Richard Wilhelm a friend who understood him through his

31. Ibid., p. 197.

32. In the Western alchemical texts it is stated that the great treasure, the "lapis philosophorum," is produced by an "opus circulatorium" or "circulatory distillation."

knowledge of Eastern wisdom. Jung never completely recovered from Wilhelm's premature death in 1930. For his part, Wilhelm was impressed by the similarity between Jung's experiences and ideas and the sayings of the Chinese text. In an article entitled "My Encounter with C. G. Jung in China" (*Neue Zürcher Zeitung*, 29 January 1929), Wilhelm says:

> There are no accidental similarities between Jung and the wisdom of the Far East, but a profound congruity of outlook on life from within. . . . Thus I have encountered Jung in China. . . . Chinese wisdom and Dr. Jung have both descended independently of one another into the depths of man's collective psyche and have there come upon realities which look so alike because they are equally anchored in the truth. This would prove that the truth can be reached from any standpoint if only one digs deep enough for it, and the congruity between the Swiss scientist and the old Chinese sages only goes to show that both are right because both have found the truth.

I shall now return to the year 1918, when Jung's active imagination came upon the mandala motif and he felt both the need and strength for scientific formulation. The first major work to appear was *Psychological Types*, in 1921. The preparations for this book go back many years,[33] probably to the time of his break with Freud.

In essence, the book is really an indirect continuation of his argument with Freud. The variety of human modes of thought and outlook is viewed from the typological standpoint, and Freud's ideas are given their rightful place. The description of the attitude and function types makes up a main part of the book. The outer or visible aspect of any one type is compensated by its own opposite, which operates from the unconscious. Here Jung broaches one of the principal

33. From the years 1915–16 there exists an extensive correspondence with his friend Dr. Hans Schmid-Guisan on the subject of typology.

themes of his scientific work: the polaristic nature of the psyche.

Psychological Types began a new creative period, which Jung described as the phase of "supplements and interpretations" of his fantasies. This was the final phase, stretching out over forty years to the day of his death. Working almost without interruption, he produced a powerful and wide-ranging body of work. This last phase did not, however, flow forth in an unbroken line: two caesuras, both connected with serious illness, became occasions for deepening and subtilizing his thought, though not for introducing any fundamental changes.

The first caesura occurred in 1944 when Jung suffered a heart attack and nearly died. In his memoirs he describes the glorious world of visionary images that opened up before him. It was another submersion in the maternal world of the collective unconscious, from which he emerged enriched after his recovery.

The visions reached their high point in the mystic marriage, the conjunction of the Cabbalistic pair Malchuth and Tifereth, the marriage of the Lamb, the hierogamy of Hera and Zeus. These visions filled Jung with indescribable bliss: "One cannot imagine the beauty and intensity of feeling during the visions. They were the most powerful things I have ever experienced."[34]

Once again these visionary images proved to be a prelude to future insights and ideas. From that time on a new aspect of the problem of opposites occupied a central place in Jung's work: he was no longer concerned with the opposition of conscious and unconscious contents, of the inner and outer worlds, of the spiritual and chthonic, so much as with a deeper penetration into the nature of the unconscious as such. In other words, he was concerned with a single sphere

34. *Memories*, p. 295.

underlying both inner and outer reality, in which the opposites are not separated from each other and individually perceptible but still constitute a paradoxical unity. The marriage vision, the *mysterium coniunctionis*, was the symbolic prefiguration of this transcendental unity.

Jung had already hinted at a transconscious, paradoxical background of the world in his alchemical studies, especially on the figure of Mercurius, whose nature unites the opposites (1942).[35] Of Mercurius the alchemists said not only that he is divine and the arcane substance but also that he is *duplex* or *utriusque capax* ("capable of both")–i.e., is spiritual and physical. In 1946 Jung took the decisive step: at his Eranos lecture he formulated his hypothesis of the *psychoid quality* of the archetype.[36] By psychoid he meant the archetype's psychic and physical nature or, as he later put it, its "neutral" nature. In this concept he expressed the conjunction of the world's great opposites.

The conception of the psychoid archetype and psychoid unconscious proved to be a fruitful working hypothesis, as in parapsychology for example. Years earlier, in 1930, Jung had demonstrated that extrasensory perceptions such as intuitions, hunches, prophetic dreams, etc. usually occur in connection with the constellation of an archetype or an archetypal situation, for example, death, illness, birth, marriage. This empirical finding now had theoretical support. From the psychological point of view, these parapsychological phenomena indicate a split in the psychoid unity of the constellated archetype. The physical component actualizes itself in the concrete event, and the psychic component in the image of this same event in a dream, intuition, or vision. Thus the same archetype appears in two essentially different manifestations and

35. Cf. "The Spirit Mercurius" (1948), *CW* 13.

36. "The Spirit of Psychology," *Eranos-Jahrbuch 1946*, later retitled "On the Nature of the Psyche," *CW* 8.

enters consciousness in this quasi-double form. Usually the inner (psychic) and outer (physical) events are separated in space and time; they come together only in the subjective experience of the individual. A dream shows here and now a faraway happening, and an intuition which occurs today perceives what will happen weeks or months from now.[37] In this telescoping of space and time, something of the original psychoid unity of the transcendent background becomes visible or subject to experience, thus explaining the feeling of mystery, wonder, or numinosity which usually accompanies these strange phenomena.

Jung's most important reflections on a unitary background, psychoid or neutral in nature, are to be found in his last major work, *Mysterium Coniunctionis*, especially in the final chapter, "The Conjunction," which for a long time he feared writing because of its formidable content. Having been stimulated by Karl Kerényi's book on the Aegean Festival in *Faust Part II*,[38] he began working on *Mysterium Coniunctionis* in his sixty-sixth year; he finished the two volumes sixteen years later.

With the hypothesis of a transcendental unitary world Jung had reached the limits of his understanding. His formulations on this subject are very cautious: "We do not know whether what we on the empirical plane regard as physical may not, in the Unknown beyond our experience, be identical with what on this side of the border we distinguish from the physical as psychic."[39] In that transcendent reality the physical and psychic seem to be identical. This thought remains, however, a postulate, since man is not in a position to make definite statements of any kind about the nature of being in its total-

37. For this reason Jung spoke not of synchronous but of synchronistic events.

38. Karl Kerényi, *Das Aegaeische Fest. Die Meergötterszene in Goethes Faust II* (Albae Vigiliae XI), 1941. Cf. *Mysterium Coniunctionis* (*CW* 14), p. xiii.

39. Ibid., §765.

ity. Jung found support, though, in a comparison between depth psychology and microphysics, a subject of numerous friendly conversations with the physicist Wolfgang Pauli. Microphysics is groping its way into the unknown mystery of matter, depth psychology into the unknown mystery of the psyche, and the two sciences have developed concepts which are remarkably analogous. This analogy has to do with the well-established relativity of time and space in those deeper psychophysical layers, and above all with the concept of complementarity. This latter concept follows from the relation between conscious and unconscious, as also from the epistemological insight that the object of investigation is only the experience or knowledge of this object but not the object itself. Pauli wrote in a letter to Jung:

> As a matter of fact the physicist would expect a psychological correspondence at this point, because the epistemological situation with regard to the concepts 'conscious' and 'unconscious' seems to offer a pretty close analogy to the 'complementarity' situation in physics. Every 'observation of the unconscious', i.e., every conscious realization of unconscious contents, has an uncontrollable reactive effect on these same contents. . . . It is undeniable that the development of 'microphysics' has brought the way in which nature is described in this science very much closer to that of the new psychology: but whereas the former, on account of the basic 'complementarity' situation, is faced with the impossibility of eliminating the effects of the observer by determinable correctives, and has therefore to abandon in principle any objective understanding of physical phenomena, the latter can supplement the purely subjective psychology of consciousness by postulating the existence of an unconscious that possesses a large measure of objective reality.[40]

Through the analogies stressed by Pauli, the hypothesis that the subject of both sciences was one and the same gained in

40. "On the Nature of the Psyche," *CW* 8, §439, n. 130.

probability. In other words, the multiplicity of the world seems to rest on a foundation of unity.

These theoretical reflections went hand in hand with investigations of a more practical psychological nature. Here the theme was the manifestation of the transcendental monocosmos in the relation between man and woman: Jung took up this question in "The Psychology of the Transference," in connection with the interpretation of an alchemical text. It appeared in 1946. Looked at psychologically, the unifying archetype of the self, operating from the transconscious sphere, wants to realize itself in the eros-smitten man and woman. This is brought about by an increasing differentiation and deepening of the relationship for which the alchemists coined the phrase "stages of conjunction." Every authentic and complete relationship is permeated by the feeling of eternity, for in the background the timeless monocosmos which has split apart is reunited in the two lovers. Jung wrote in a letter (in English): "The living mystery of life is always hidden between Two, and it is the true mystery which cannot be betrayed by words or depleted by arguments" (12 August 1960).

The confrontation with the paradoxical monocosmos finally led Jung to a decisive step in his psychology of religion. Fundamentally, his entire work is to be understood as a psycho-religious statement, a progressive interpretation of the numinous by which man is consciously or unconsciously filled, surrounded, and led. "My lifework is essentially an attempt to understand what others apparently can believe" (letter, 21 May 1948).

The problem of opposites had played a role in his religious writings from the beginning. I can only touch on it here. On the one hand, it had to do with his reflections on Jesus and the Devil, on the other with Jesus and the alchemical *lapis*. In this connection he tended to elevate into the sphere of the

Divine the feminine, dark, chthonic aspect which he found in the unconscious of modern man. This numen contradicted the trinitarian God-image but, by adding a fourth dominant, turned it into a divine quaternity, a symbol of wholeness. This religious aspect of the problem of opposites grew out of his interpretation of historical documents and above all out of the religious experiences of modern men, who do not always think in terms of dogmatic formulations. Jung first dealt with these facts and ideas in *Psychology and Religion*; it appeared in 1937, several years before the caesuras of the last creative period.

Only much later did another aspect of the problem of opposites come to the fore. It was no longer the antagonistic, complementary, and more or less independent dominants but rather an original polarity in the God-image as such, particularly the God-image of the Old and New Testaments. From a psychological point of view, a God-image is nearer the unutterable, mysterious ground of the psyche and the world the more clearly we can perceive its intrinsic paradoxicality, i.e., the more strongly its immanent contrariety stands out. At bottom one then finds the chthonic and spiritual in one and the same God-image: light beside darkness, creative power beside destructive will, goodness and love beside anger and injustice.

For a long while Jung shrank from giving definite formulation to such contrariety in the Judaeo–Christian God-image. He was aware that through the critique of the image of a just and good God he would be injuring an ancient and deeply rooted tradition. But he also knew that in every age there were records of pious men who had not shrunk back before the vision of the dark side of the God-image; indeed, such features were even mentioned in the Old and New Testaments. In the midst of this conflict, Jung, now seventy-six years old, once more fell seriously ill—this is the second caesura in his final creative phase. In a fever he wrote down his *Answer to Job*, as if from inner dictation. "If there is anything like the spirit seizing one by the scruff of the neck, it was the way this book came into being," he wrote in a letter (17 July 1951).

Answer to Job is the psychological exegesis of a Biblical text, but also a confession, and this accounts for its passion. The confessional nature of the book is affirmed in a letter Jung wrote in February 1954 to an English clergyman who had discussed *Answer to Job*:

> The attribute 'coarse' is mild in comparison to what you feel when God dislocates your hip or when he slays the first-born. I bet Jacob's punches he handed to the angel were not just caresses or polite gestures. They were of the good hard kind; as you rightly say, 'with the gloves off'.—That is *one side* of my experience with what is called 'God'. 'Coarse' is too weak a word for it. 'Crude', 'violent', 'cruel', 'bloody', 'hellish', 'demonic' would be better. That I was not downright blasphemous I owe to my domestication and polite cowardice. And at every step I felt hindered by a beatific vision of which I'd better say nothing.

One may regret Jung's reticence, but anything else was unthinkable considering his faithfulness to his work, which was written under the spell of the "spirit of the depths." One recalls the phallic daimon who, long ago, had claimed his rights in that childhood dream. The preponderance of darkness remained the decisive factor in Jung's work to the end of his life; it also determined his attitude to that unspeakable transcendental power named God. "One *can* love God, and *must* fear him."[41]

But the more deeply Jung penetrated into the enigmatic world of the unconscious and the more strongly he sensed the numinosity of the dark powers, the more clearly he acknowl-

41. "Answer to Job," *CW* 11, §733.

edged the value of reflective consciousness as a gift of perception and understanding granted to mankind. This in no way contradicts an opus dedicated to the "spirit of the depths"; only by virtue of an equally powerful, incorruptible, and courageous consciousness could it take shape at all. Consciousness is the supreme virtue, for it directs awareness to the existence of the inner and outer worlds, the light and dark worlds, and in this way clothes them with reality. Jung spoke in his later years of the "miracle of reflecting consciousness"[42] and of the "cosmic meaning of consciousness."[43] Formulated in religious language: "Man is the mirror which God holds up before him, or the sense organ with which he apprehends his being" (letter, 28 March 1953).

At first Jung saw the source of creativity in the unconscious and its autonomous powers. In old age, he lay prime stress on the creative resonance of a consciousness that stands firm against the onslaught of the unconscious and does not falter when something incomprehensible happens. In apprehending, it creates reality, even if it halts before the inexplicable and leaves the mysteries of life unquestioned. Consciousness has, however, another aspect: apprehending the world and ourselves and knowing of the polaristic nature of the psyche compel us to adopt a more reflective and modest attitude toward life, and especially a more tolerant attitude toward our fellow men. Consciousness becomes an ethical challenge arising from within; great responsibility is laid upon the individual, but it also endows him with real human worth.

Today more than ever it is obvious that life itself is dependent upon the responsible consciousness of every individual. The unconsciousness of human beings and their submergence in a more or less irresponsible mass disturbed Jung deeply and cast a shadow over his last years. With apprehension he saw the dangers which arise when the truth of the depths is

42. *Memories*, p. 339.
43. Ibid., p. 255.

not recognized, its darkness neither endured nor enlightened. Above all he foresaw catastrophes threatening the existence of the human species. Too few listened to him or understood the issues. Despite all worldly honors, Jung felt himself the voice of one crying in the wilderness. Sadness and apprehension are echoed in the prophetic words of the seer:

> It is not presumption that drives me, but my conscience as a psychiatrist that bids me fulfil my duty and prepare those few who will hear me for coming events which are in accord with the end of an era. . . . I am, to be quite frank, concerned for all those who are caught unprepared by the events in question and disconcerted by their incomprehensible nature.[44]

What Jung had to offer against the pressing dangers was not a recommendation for the governance of groups or nations but always greater consciousness, painfully achieved and difficult to endure, on the part of the individual, or of many individuals. "The whole future, the whole history of the world, ultimately springs as a gigantic summation from these hidden sources in individuals. In our own most private and subjective lives we are not only the passive witnesses of our age, and its sufferers, but also its makers. We make our epoch."[45] Thus, also, "a change in the attitude of the individual can bring about a renewal in the spirit of the nations."[46] Creativity is maintained as a counterweight if every advance in the knowledge and mastery of the outer world is compensated by an ever more passionate regard for the spirit of the depths, or of the unconscious.[47] In the face of the unprecedented possibil-

44. "Flying Saucers: A Modern Myth," *CW* 10, §389–90.
45. "The Meaning of Psychology for Modern Man," *CW* 10, §315.
46. "Epilogue to 'Essays on Contemporary Events,'" *CW* 10, §459.
47. Wolfgang Pauli asserts that in the area of natural science a corresponding archetypal image must underlie every conceptual formulation. Cf. "The Influence of Archetypal Ideas on the Scientific Theories of Kepler," in Jung–Pauli, *The Interpretation of Nature and the Psyche* (London and New York, 1955). In the area of political life, consciousness of the shadow is essential in order to avoid the pernicious projections of evil.

ities of space travel, biological manipulation, and the total annihilation of life on our planet, consciousness and conscience must be deepened proportionately to prevent man's god-almightiness from striking out in destruction and bringing down catastrophe on the heads of us all. In view of the mass-mindedness of contemporary humanity, Jung was sceptical of the chances of any such psychological development and was oppressed by his knowledge of the autonomous explosions that may at any moment be sparked off in the depths and wipe out the human race. "The world today," he said in 1957, "hangs by a thin thread, and that is the psyche of man."[48]

Even in old age Jung was never the wise man standing above life, which he loved and knew how to enjoy. His wisdom was of a different kind: it was the wisdom of a man who had looked deep into the human heart, including his own, but suffered under the enormous paradoxicality of existence. His attitude toward his own death, also, was not one of detached acceptance. He complained very humanly about the brutality of old age, which drained him of his powers one by one. But he had discovered that the psyche reaches out into a sphere of timelessness, and so he came to the conviction that it does not end even in death. Although he relegated his thoughts on this subject to the area of "mythologizing," they granted him inner peace.

Concerning his work, he had the feeling at the end of his life that he had done and said everything in his power. Four months before his death, in his eighty-sixth year, he wrote in a letter: "I can only remark that every single book was written with all the responsibility I could muster, that I was honest, and have presented facts which in themselves are not out of date. I would not wish any of my publications undone and I stand by everything I have said."

48. Interview with Richard I. Evans in 1957. Cf. Evans, *Conversations with Carl Jung* (Princeton: Van Nostrand, 1964), p. 17.